To Our dear
from '|
and
Oludayomis
Happy Reading
Dec 2022.

ALL ABOUT LIFE

The Beginning, the ending of time
and all that's needed in between

Adejoke Oludayomi

ACKNOWLEDGEMENTS

This is my fifth book and it is dedicated to everyone who have read my write ups in magazines, blogs, bulletins or other social media technologies at one time or the other over the past twenty odd years. Thank you for your encouragement.

Here's hoping you'll enjoy being reminded about some of them as you read come across some of them again in this book.
I did.

Contents

PROLOGUE
THE DATELESS PAST

The serenity of heaven is broken.

The sounds emanating have never been heard before. What sound is that? There has only and always been peace in heaven. Now they hear the sound of battle. The sound of war. Forceful upheavals on every side.

Angels dashing here and there their bright shining dazzling appearances now appear to be on fire. The lesser angels are bewildered.

"What could be happening?" they wonder. Looking for answers from their superiors, they get none.

The brightness of the atmosphere notwithstanding, a feel of apprehension fills the air.

They are not kept in silence for much longer as the voice of God, the Creator Jehovah the LORD of all booms across the heavens.

Judgement is being mete out. And though it was in the court room of Jehovah, you were allowed to hear it all across heaven.

"Judgement is hereby being delivered to you, Lucifer, formerly known as Son of the Morning and the following angels under your command".

As the names of countless angels were being reeled out, gasps of surprise and dismay escaped from the lips of the angels listening as they recognised fellow cherubs of God being condemned.

""Now you are cut down to the ground and cast out of heaven. For you have said in your heart: "I will ascend into heaven, I will exalt my throne above the stars of God; I will also sit on the mount of the congregation on the farthest sides of the north; I will ascend above the heights of the clouds, I will be like the Most High.""

Even as the Almighty LORD God Jehovah utters His words, screeches and howls of a devilish sort burst out and fill the tranquillity of the heavens.

"Instead, you shall be brought down to Sheol, to the lowest depths of hell, prepared for you to be confined in the fullness of time and forever."

Suddenly as the mighty Arch angel, Michael and the warring angels under his command appear, before everyone's eyes, the erstwhile bright and glorious form of the rebellious angels begins to dim and fade. Soon they turn dull gold, grey and then almost completely black. Their features change and what was a beautiful sight to look upon before, immediately turns into a hideous ugly caricature of a being. And the putrefying odour that poured out from them which had never been experienced in heaven before now, starts to nauseate the onlooking angels.

Who knew angels could smell? There was no need to. The aroma of the presence of God ensured that they never needed to. But now the stench of angels going through the process of corruption filled the air.

Who knew the boundaries of heaven? Who knew you could be thrown out? Who knew there was a place called "hell?"

As if in answer to the thoughts of alarm raging through the onlooking angels, Arch angel, Gabriel, the LORD's most trusted messenger replies.

"It never existed before. Hell has just been created for Lucifer and his rebellious angels. It is a place of torment, fire and punishment and all who defy and disobey the LORD, will eventually be sent there, never to be released." His explanation also serves as a strong warning. His piercing eyes seem to go through them as if to ask them if they would desire to visit the place themselves.

"No. Never", they shudder, as the piercing screams of the angels turned demons fade as they are all cast into the depths of hell.

Lucifer, the anointed cherub that covered the presence of the Almighty God, was the last to be cast out. Beautifully made and crafted by the hands of God Himself, all angels secretly envied him.

Every precious stone was his covering, the sardius, topaz, and the diamond, the beryl, the onyx, and the jasper, the sapphire, the emerald, and the carbuncle, and gold. Musical instruments were worked into his frame on the day he was created. He walked up and down the holy mountain of God; He walked through the stones of fire. He was perfect in all his ways until he became proud and lifted up in himself. His heart was lifted up because of his beauty and wisdom and one day he decided to try and overthrow God, Himself.

Of course, he would always fail.
But now even in his disgrace, he is unrepentant and without remorse. As he is cast out of God's presence he defiantly lifts his fist and shouts, "It is not over yet. The fight is still on!"

And Jehovah LORD of lords, Creator and King of all, replies quietly and regally, "We will see."

CHAPTER ONE
THE BEGINNING.

The whole host of heaven watched in trepidation, wishing, hoping, praying that she wouldn't listen to him. But she does. And then in great horror they watch as she reaches out, picks the fruit and takes the deadly bite.

"Eat it, she offers her husband with her, "It'll make us equal with God".

They eat and just as the Creator had warned, they both begin to age. Their bodies feel heavy. Their eyes seem dim. Adam begins to cough, something he had never done before. A new strange emotion overwhelms them. Fear rises up and envelopes them. They look around. Everything kind of looks different. All of a sudden it seems that the animals are not as friendly and as tame as before.

Can they hear treacherous evil laughter in the garden? They sow fig leaves together as they realise that the glory covering of the Creator Father God has departed from them. By the end of the day they begin to suffer His anger and disappointment for they have aligned themselves with His arch enemy … bound to him for ever.

Heaven is sad that night. The Father's precious much loved children have sinned and the wages of sin is death. It's the Word of God. Cannot be changed. Cannot be broken. All is lost. Man and his descendants are lost forever. Committing the same sin that the arch angel Lucifer had committed. Wanting to rule like God. Wanting to be like God. Now waiting to bear the same punishment meted out to him. An eternity in hell. Always and forever separated from their heavenly Father God.

Heaven is indeed sad that night. The heart of the Father God is heavy, but He is LOVE and love still moves Him.

"I must save them from the clutches of the evil one," He declares

"But how? Can there be a way out? The wages of sin…"

"…Is death", the Father completes the silent question in the mind of all the host of heavenly beings present in that court room. "It is My Word and can never be broken. It can never be changed. Death must follow sin. And because of that, Someone will have to die …. for them… in their place. A man just like them. But He must be an innocent, pure, sinless man. Yes, I will punish that Man instead of them and judgement would have been rightly served".

"But where will You find such a man?"
"Does such a man exist?"
"The sin nature in Adam will pass down through his generations. In Adam all men will sin. All men will die. None will be clean. None can be pure."

The questions evolve from all over the court room.
"Someone needs to go from here". The Creator God looks around the room.

Everyone is silent. To exchange their powerful stately spiritual bodies for the weak and dying frame of a man? Every angel's head is bowed down, every tongue is still. No one is ready to go and pay that awesome sacrifice.

After a long silence they all rise to their feet in awe as the Voice of the Creator God decides.

"I, Myself will go down, in the form of MY WORD. I will become the Man they will come to know as JESUS. I will give Myself up to be punished. I will surrender Myself to die in their stead. I will pour out My blood. With My blood I will reconcile them back to Myself. And as many as accept My death and sacrifice, will once more become what they were destined and created to be, My sons...the SONS OF GOD.

CHAPTER TWO
THE PLAN

They watched the Creator God in great awe, as Someone separated Himself from inside of Him. The beautiful shinning Being stood apart from the Creator God. They could tell He was obviously a part of God and yet somehow different.

As the Creator and His Son smile at each other, the Creator explains.
"He has always been with Me and in Me. We are One. He is the Manifestation of My Word. He is a part of Me that no one knows exists and it is by Him that the world was created and by Him mankind will be redeemed."
As all the host watch, the Creator God continues.

"He will be known as Yeshua HaMashiach in the Hebrew language but down the ages, different cultures and languages will call Him in their native tongue. In some countries, for instance, He'll be known as Jesus. All interpretations mean "I, Jehovah saves.""

"Now we have a Saviour, we need to find a body. It is via the normal human reproductive process that My Word will enter into the world. The Man must be born of a woman to be truly human".

As the Creator looks ahead into time, He makes His choice. A woman highly favoured by Him, crafted by Him and approved by Him even before she was born, to be the vessel by which the Saviour, now Spirit will become a man, of flesh.

"Her name will be Mary, of Jewish descent. A descendant daughter of Abraham. A man who will be called My friend. She will be the Saviour's earthly mother. She is the one I have chosen".

And so, the ages unfold. Adam fathers Seth, born to continue the line of the Messiah after Cain killed the accepted brother, Abel. Enoch, Noah down to Abraham. Mankind groans under the oppression of the evil lord Satan and his cohorts, and heaven waits for the exact time of their deliverance.

Isaac, Jacob, his sons, the 12 patriarchs are born, live out their lives and die.

Slavery in Egypt begins and after 430 years of living there, Moses, great prophet of God, leads God's people to freedom and their slavery comes to an end. They conquer and take possession of the land promised to their fathers. Yet they are still under the power of sin.

Joshua, Deborah, Samson, Gideon, judges appointed by God to rule His people, they all come and go.
David, great grandson of Ruth the Moabitess and Boaz, a type of a kinsman redeemer, is born. Samuel another great prophet of God, consecrates David, who goes down in history as Israel's greatest king, a man after God's own heart.

Still the Creator God watches and waits for the right time for the Messiah to appear.

Heaven looks on as the Kingdom of Israel divides into two and see the emergence of all manner of good and wicked kings. Sin increases amongst men and they turn away from God the Creator. As a result, He leaves them at the mercy of their enemies. They are constantly defeated at war and taken into captivity.

Yet even in captivity there's always a remnant who serve God at the risk of their lives. Daniel,

Shadrach, Meshach, Abednego and a host of other men and women who were willing to give up their lives as martyrs in honour of the God they loved and served.

Though God's children do eventually return to their promised land, they cannot remain faithful to God. Their souls are in bondage to Satan and they are unable to do what is right. Hearts seared, nature changed, they always do wickedly. They can't help themselves. They need a Saviour.

The most wicked of all their oppressors eventually overrides them. The iron fisted Roman Empire. He rules over them with tyranny and terror. He defiles and enslaves their maidens and spills the blood of their young men on wooden crosses.

The host of heaven silently ask "When? Oh LORD, just and true, will You not deliver Your people from the throes of suffering and death?"

The Ancient of Days, the Creator God still watches and………waits.

CHAPTER THREE
THE DESCENT

And so, the Creator God keeps the watch and the wait until…

"It is time. The time appointed is here. Man's redemption is at hand" He declares.

"The Messiah will have no earthly father and so He will be free from the sinful nature passed on from human fathers to their sons and daughters. He will carry My nature, the holy nature of His heavenly Father but will still have to make the decision to obey Me, be faithful to Me and to keep My commandments."

Addressing His Word directly He says solemnly, "Man's eternal destiny depends on You, My Son. I know You will not fail. We cannot afford for You to fail."

The host of heaven marvel at the mystery of a Being equal in power, authority and strength, being a part of the Creator Father God and yet acting in complete submission to Him. The rebellion of Lucifer is still fresh in their minds, a created being who chose to struggle with His Creator for the power that could never belong to Him. Would this be different? Would the Word remain subject to the Father in this assignment given to Him or would He also follow the way of Adam, the very man He has gone to redeem? Time would tell.

The Word stands silent in the presence of the Creator Father God. He needs not give an audible reply, for they know and read Each other's thoughts but for the benefit of the heavenly hosts, He chooses to use the same medium as was used to address Him.

"I am ready, Father, I will not fail".

"The assignment begins" announces the Father God, as Gabriel the trusted arch angel, lifts His wings and begins his flight down to earth, to a little town in Israel called Nazareth to locate the abode of the chosen virgin, Mary.

In what seems like the twinkling of an eye, He is back standing in front of the throne of the Father.

"She has been told and she waits in obedience for the performance of what she has been chosen to do, my LORD".

The Creator Father addresses the heavenly court again.

"My Spirit will go with Him and make a way for Him to enter and to incubate in Mary's womb. For the human time frame of 9 months will He be hidden after which He will be born, as all men after Adam, have been and will always be, of a woman. Thus, He will be God but also man".

"He will cry like a man. Learn obedience to His parents like a man. He will hunger and thirst as men do. He will love, be glad and sorrow just like a man. Flesh and blood, He will have, as so He will feel pain like men do. He will go down to reconcile man back to Me.

"But will they believe Him, Holy, Holy, Holy One?" they ask from all over the room.

"Some will," the Father replies. "Some will but not all. But as many as believe in Him, Africans, Asians, Caucasians, and those who are of mixed races, if they choose to accept Him and His death as a ransom for their lives, they will be free from eternal death and be reconciled to Me forever".

"And now the mystery of the plan is hidden from the minds of any and all whom would seek to thwart or hinder it. For in the fullness of time, the Man Jesus will die a painful gruesome death, at the hand of men, in the place of all men.
They will not know the fullness of its power. Though they will try to war against it, in their human foolishness and futility, they will only inadvertently be working for it."

So, we end the saga in this chapter, as the Word descends from the heavens to mysteriously become a foetus in the womb of a peasant woman Mary, God Himself becoming a man to buy back His beloved creation and elevating them from created beings to sons and daughters of God. That is, for anyone who will endeavour to receive that offer.

Will you?

CHAPTER FOUR
THE BIRTH

It is 9 months later, by earth's time and heaven is looking down into the city of Nazareth as the Chosen Seed of Abraham grows in the womb of Mary to full time. Everyone is excited. You can even feel the sense of anticipation around the Father God even though He knows all things from their beginning right up till their end. Mankind's redemption is on course and the stage is ready.

"But how will she know that The Messiah is to be born in Bethlehem, O God, faithful and true? She is heavy with Child and still resides in Nazareth. The prophecy from the mouth of Your prophet, Micah hails Bethlehem Ephrathah, too little to be among the clans of Judah, as the birth place of the Messiah. It is from whom shall come forth for the LORD One who is to be ruler in Israel, whose coming forth is from of old, from ancient days."

The Father God smiles at Gabriel, the arch angel.

"You have a keen eye and a sharp memory. I formed you well."

He continues.

"The heart of kings are in the palm of My hands and I am turning the heart of Caesar Augustus to count the people for taxation purposes. All will return to their home towns…"

"…And Joseph and Mary are from the town of Bethlehem, the city of David," finishes the arch angel. "They obey the decree, not even realising that it is You, O Wise and Holy One that is actually leading and directing their steps. It's all in Your plan that the scripture, Your eternal Word might be fulfilled."

So it was, that, while Joseph and Mary were at Bethlehem for the census, the days were accomplished that Mary should be delivered. She brought forth her firstborn son, and wrapped Him in swaddling clothes, and laid Him in a manger; because there was no room for them in the inn. On that awesome night the hosts of heaven join the lowly shepherds singing, "Hosanna! Peace on earth. Goodwill to all men. Glory to our God in the highest!"

CHAPTER FIVE
THE ENEMY

As heaven rejoiced in elation, another audience looked on in fear, anger and trepidation. Not all spiritual beings rejoiced in the fulfilment of prophecy of the Saviour Messiah. Evil eyes watched, demonic grunts could be heard from the dark plain of Hades known also as Sheol – the place of death.

"The magi come from afar to worship the Jewish king." "The prophecy seems to be unravelling right before our eyes. It looks like Yahweh has put a plan of redemption in process."

"This new born boy seems to be more special than any child born before."

"Even more special than the great Moses, the deliverer."

The evil voices emanate from all around, piercing the darkness of hell, the resident abode of the evil lord, Satan.

"Who dares call any human special in my presence!" roars the once anointed cherub that had at one time covered the presence of the Almighty God, Himself.

"Man is fallen, lost forever. I rule the universe now and I will rule forever. Nothing can change that. Man belongs to me. He will never be free. NEVER!!"

"But what will you do, lord of all fallen beings?" the question resounding across the dark and dismal abode of diverse sorts of evil, perverted unclean spirits.

"The same strategy I always use! Steal, kill and destroy. That is my name and that's the rule of my game."

Evil demonic laughter roars out of this wicked and malevolent spirit. Once highly revered and respected. Once the trusted right hand angel. All angels admired and envied his exalted position. A created being yet lifted to a position of being in the glorious presence of the Great and Holy Ancient of Days. Eli, the Creator of all. But alas pride, arrogance and insurgency was found in and took over, him. He dared…yes, he dared to rebel against the One who holds the heavens and the earth in the palm of His hands. The Great and Mighty YAHWEH, the LORD, JEHOVAH himself.

Why he believed he could dethrone the un-dethrone -able One, only God who sees and knows the inward parts of all creation, can ever tell. But he chose to destroy his own destiny, the destiny of a third of the hosts of heaven with him and of course, the destiny of the much loved chosen species called Man. Even now he is still hell bent on devastating and totally annihilating the purpose of God for man's redemption.

Is heaven unaware of his devises and evil intentions? Of course not!

The Great and Mighty LORD Jehovah looks on at the scene from His high throne in the heavens, as the evil ruler Satan strategizes his wicked plan.

"The so called new born King is still a mere man, a feeble babe, flesh and bones," Satan declares. "What I engineered thousands of earth years before in the land of Egypt, the killing of the new born male child, I will do again. No man will deliver mankind from my hands. They, their children and their generations yet to be born all belong to me, Satan, lord of darkness. Their lives, their souls, their bodies, their inheritance…all is mine…forever and ever. Let the slaughter of the babies in Judea begin!!!"

He cries out as He summons the demon in charge of genocide. This evil demon power was the same one who possessed Pharoah of Egypt centuries before in an attempt to curtail the increase of the children of Israel in Egypt.

Once more he is given the evil task of possessing, Herod the king who ruled over Judea to move Him to once again murder countless baby boys on earth.

And so here we leave the continuing saga of the redemption of man as the thunderous deafening roar of war and agreement resounds from the fallen angels through the dark corridors of hell. The ranks of the devil's army stand in hail of their evil master. "We will thwart the plans of Jehovah. We will always rule over man," they scream in devilish glee.

And Jehovah, the Great and Mighty God, the Ancient of Days who sees all things and knows all things, listens and watches from the heavens, knowing that their evil plans to stop the redemption of man would always fail.

CHAPTER SIX
THE WORK

And so the plan of Jehovah continues to unfold.

The baby Jesus grows to be a boy, a teenager and then a young man. His mother Mary, never forgot the visit of the angel. The visit of the shepherds and the wise men from the East, seemed like a distant memory now. But she knew every time she looked at Him that He was a special child.

Always obedient, caring and a wonderful role model to his siblings He was a joy to be around and she was so proud to be His mother. But she knew in her spirit that the time of His appearing was at hand. He would soon leave her…even if it was only for a season, she knew it would be hard.

With a twinge of sadness she remembers the frightening prophecy of the aged prophetess Anna years ago, "a sword shall pierce through your soul also".
Whatever may come and whatever she had to endure the LORD Himself would help her go through. His will be done.

The boy Jesus becomes a man and at the prime age of thirty, He starts His ministry.

The LORD God sends His Spirit to baptise and empower Him. He chooses His disciples, ordinary men like you and me to help Him in the work. Fishermen, tax collectors, a doctor, lawyer, men and women who God had made available to help Him in His quest to reconcile man to God and to help prepare Him for the awesome sacrifice He had been born to make.

For three and a half years He goes about doing good. Healing the sick, cleansing lepers, opening the eyes of the blind, giving life to paralysed limbs so the lame and paralytics rise up and walk. He stills the storms of life both physical and spiritual. He casts out demons and gives mad men their lives back again. Kind and compassionate He weeps for men and their lost position in God. Not coming to judge or condemn He says men and women from the harsh consequences of breaking the law and tells them to "Go and sin no more". The Son of God Himself, sometimes He has no roof over His head and not much money in His purse, yet He gives freely to the poor and brings joy to the down and out and the broken hearted.

He fasts, prays and works tirelessly as He knows He doesn't have much time. He freely gives. He freely loves. He freely empties out Himself.

Jarius' daughter remembers Him. Lazarus remembers Him. The widow of Nain's son remembers Him for it is He who raised them from the dead.

Multitudes throng Him and walk miles and miles to sit and hear Him teach and preach about the kingdom of God. Thousands love Him but so many also hate Him.

The religious rulers of the day believe Him to be a threat to their very existence. The felt He would anger the Romans who ruled over them then. Or could it be that they knew deep inside that this new movement of love, peace, signs and wonders would take over and they would become history.

Anyway, they plot to exterminate Him.

All is in God's plan.

And at last it was fulfilled as God had purposed.

Jesus, Son of God, also known as Emmanuel, is betrayed by one of His disciples for thirty pieces of silver.

After a kangaroo court trial, He is scourged to an inch of His life and nailed to a wooden cross at Golgotha, Calvary. His blood pouring out, He cries out with a loud voice, "It is finished" and gives up the ghost.

And to all who are watching on earth, in heaven and in hell, it seems that it is indeed, all over.

CHAPTER SEVEN
DEAD OR ALIVE?

It is a dark and cold weary night. It seems that all is lost. Deep sorrow, a long painful lingering sadness fills the atmosphere. Everything we had built our hopes on … has come crashing down at our feet. How could this be?

We thought finally our victory had come. We would be restored as a nation to the glorious existence of old. Our men would take their rightful place in the government of our land. Our women beautifully adorned in our homes, free of oppression, liberated to live fruitful and peaceful lives.

It was at our finger tips. We only needed to reach out and take it.

We saw His naked demonstration of power. Blind eyes popped open. The lame walked. Demons fled at His presence. The stinking curse of leprosy dissolved into brand new baby like skin. We revelled in the euphoria of the oncoming victory we anticipated in Him.

But alas it was not to be. His own people delivered Him up to the Romans, for no reason at all. An innocent Lamb… sacrificed, battered, broken and crucified on a rugged jaggered cross. We heard Him cry out, "It is finished!" and truly it was … over. For He was dead and gone.

Or so we thought.

Until late on Sunday evening as we travelled down from Jerusalem along the dusty road to Emmaus, hearts filled with sorrow, our souls almost irreparably damaged, Someone strode up and walked in step with us. At first, we thought He was a Stranger in these parts for He didn't seem to know what had transpired over the last couple of days. But then He began to speak to us and lo and behold, His very Words blazed like a shot of lightening through our hearts.

He began to remind us of what the ancient scriptures had said about the Messiah, the Saviour of men. How it had been written that He would die in the place of sinful men to reconcile them back to their God.

He began to expound the scriptures from the book of Genesis up till Malachi showing us the prophecies of the Messiah in each one.

He assured us that contrary to what we thought, Jesus Christ, the Messiah was not dead, but alive for evermore. In Him and with Him, all men have the complete and eternal victory.

Then He reassured us. "Just remain connected, bound and attached, and truly you will have that victory!"

As we arrived at home we begged Him to stay the night as it was quite dark outside. We just could not allow Him to go on. There was something about Him.

And then when we sat at supper, He took bread, broke it and immediately our eyes were opened. As He vanished from our sight, we knew that our hearts had burned within us as we walked together along the way because it was Jesus, our LORD.

CHAPTER EIGHT
TWO ON THE ROAD TO EMMAUS

The synopsis of the story is as follows. Jesus had just died a horrible gruesome death on a jaggered cross at Calvary. Stories were going around that He had somehow resurrected. But it was just too much to believe. There was sadness and disappointment amongst His disciples and the rest of His followers. They wondered about all they had supposed and hoped that He would do for them and now it seemed all hope was gone and the promises were not going to be fulfilled after all.

Verses 21-24 But we were hoping that it was He who was going to redeem Israel. Indeed, besides all this, today is the third day since these things happened. Yes, and certain women of our company, who arrived at the tomb early, astonished us when they did not find His body, they came saying that they had also seen a vision of angels who said He was alive and certain of us who were with us went to the tomb and found it just as the women had said; but Him they did not see.

What truths are hidden in these twenty-three verses that we can be enlightened by this today?

- **Where two or three are gathered together in My name, there I am in the midst of them**.

Verses 14 & 15: And they talked together of all these things which had happened. So it was, while they conversed and reasoned, that Jesus Himself drew near and went with them.

Our God is omnipresent. Not only is He present when we speak about Him, He's also there when we pray or worship Him. When and wherever we are honouring Him, He is present. "Lo I am with you always," He promises, "Even until the end of the age." Whenever His name is being mentioned, spoken in prayer or cried out to in times of distress or danger, He is there. In time of rejoicing, in times of sorrow, beloved the omnipresent LORD is always present.

- **When Jesus asks a question is not that He doesn't know the answer**

In verse 17, Jesus asks the two on the road to Emmaus, "What kind of conversation *is* this that you have with one another as you walk and are sad?" Then the one whose name was Cleopas answered and said to Him, "Are You the only stranger in Jerusalem, and have You not known the things which happened there in these days?"

And He said to them, "What things?"

They said to Him, "The things concerning Jesus of Nazareth, who was a Prophet mighty in deed and word before God and all the people…

Did Jesus know what they were saying among themselves? Of course, He did.

In the garden of Eden, God called out for Adam after the eating of the forbidden fruit, "Adam where are you"? He knew what had transpired and He knew where Adam was. Yet He still asked. "Cain, where is Abel, your brother?" He asked in Genesis 4:9. He knew Cain had killed his brother but He still asked.

"What is your name?" He asked the band of demons entrenched in the mad man at Gardara, (Mark 5:1-20)

He knew who they were. He created them long ago as good angels, ministering spirits of God. He knew them from the time they came to be, when they rebelled and even right at the time when they were about to be cast out.

"What do you want Me to do for you?" Jesus asked the obviously blind Bartimaeus, He knew the man was blind. He was sitting by the wayside begging.

So why then does He ask you the question?

Because beloved, He wants you to affirm or confirm what you want, what you need, what you desire. He wants you to be specific.. Go straight to the point. Don't beat about the bush. Don't moan, grumble or complain. Tell is as it is. "This is how I feel, LORD. This is what I need. I am troubled by this or that". He knows already but He still wants you to tell Him. He wants to converse with you.

- **Jesus can restrain eyes from seeing**

In verse 16, their eyes were restrained. They saw Him but didn't recognise Him. Jesus has the power to open the eyes of the blind, to give inward sight or vision to those who seek it but He can also restrain eyes from seeing.

Though Elisha could see them clearly, his servant needed to have his eyes opened to see the hosts of God's army protecting them when Syrian army came to arrest his master.

Isaiah 6:10. "Make the heart of this people dull, and their ears heavy…shut their eyes Lest they see with their eyes, And hear with their ears, And understand with their heart, And return and be healed."

Yikes! Why would you want to do that LORD? "For a time… He replies in the following verse. "Until I have accomplished what I choose." Our prayer is to be able to see beyond the natural, what others cannot see. May the eyes of our understanding be enlightened and may we not be like the Pharisees, "The blind leading the blind into the ditch."

Open my eyes O LORD that I may see what I need to see, to fulfil my destiny.

CHAPTER NINE
TWO STILL ON THE ROAD TO EMMAUS

Luke 24:13-35

Jesus had told His disciples that He would die and rise again. They didn't want it to happen but He had said beforehand that He had come to Jerusalem for just that purpose. Nevertheless, when the word of God by the prophets was fulfilled, the two on the road to Emmaus could not recognise it. They could not believe. Jesus called them void of understanding and slow to believe in all that the prophets had spoken. What that means is that when we act in   ignorance of the word of God and its implications for us and our families, we also act foolishly and without understanding.

My people are destroyed for lack of knowledge, Hosea 4:6 says. **My people**, not unbelievers, not sinners, not back sliders…My people. Maybe if the followers of Jesus had believed the foretelling of the passion of their LORD, it might have been a little bit less traumatic and devastatingly hopeless as it eventually became to them. They would have still gone through the trial and the testing, yes, but hope would have been a reassuring peaceful spring of waters for them as they passed through the fiery furnace. They would've waited in expectancy for the resurrection of their LORD.

For when we pass through the fire, Isaiah 43:1&2; we should remember that it will not burn us. God will not go contrary to His Word. What are you passing through? What fire? What flood? What wilderness? What mountain are we trying to climb? What has God said concerning it? Listen. Read the relevant word. Memorise it. Learn it by heart. Stand on it. It can never fail.

- In verses 28 & 29 He made as if He would go further but they constrained Him to stay.

Sometimes the visitation of the LORD is by invitation.

We invite Him into our hearts, lives and situations. "Lo I stand at the door and knock," He beckons to us in Revelation 3:20. He knocks, we open.

Sometimes however, the LORD initiates the invitation.

"Zacchaeus," He calls out in Luke 19:1-5 to the spiritually hungry man who climbs the sycamore tree to catch a glimpse of Him passing by. "Come down, I'm coming to your house today!"

Those who hunger and thirst after righteousness shall be filled. Matthew 5:6 and as the deer pants for the water brooks, so I pant also for you my LORD.

- Cleopas and his companion (might have been a friend, or his wife) recognised that there "is something about this Stranger.

"Did not our hearts burn within us while He talked with us on the road?" they wondered.

What effect do we have on people we meet or come in contact with? Do people feel refreshed after an encounter with us or do we leave them with a bad sour taste in their mouths? Do we lift up people's spirits or do we pull them down? Words are powerful. Jesus said, "The words that I speak they are spirit and they are life". Words can build up. Words can crush a spirit. What are we doing with the power embedded in our tongues? Lifting up or destroying?

When Jesus called them, "Oh foolish ones", notice that they were not offended. Even when truth is to be spoken, it must be in love. Rebuke must never be done in haste, but in quiet reflection and with the help of the Holy Spirit. We need to get the right words and into the right atmosphere in order to get the right effect and result. The love, truth and compassion emanating from Jesus swallowed up any bad feeling those two might otherwise have felt. Let's choose our words wisely and allow Jesus be seen and felt in us, at all times.

- The power of the Holy Communion

Finally, Jesus took bread and after blessing it, He broke it and gave it to them. Then their eyes were opened. Communion with the Lamb of God has the power to do the extraordinary in our lives. One of which is to open our eyes that we may see beyond the natural, beyond our present circumstances. Jesus said "When you eat of my body and drink of my flesh, you'll have life in you." Light will shine through your darkness. Darkness must flee before the light of God's revelation. Everything hitherto hidden from you will be revealed or exposed.

Go and partake of the Holy Communion with Jesus. He will give you deep insight and solution to that problem. Bread, prophetically is the doctrine of the word. It also symbolises deliverance. It also stands for healing of the body, soul and spirit. We need all these and more and can receive them at the table of our LORD. Don't stay back. Reach out and receive what has been wrought for you at Calvary.

Jesus Christ, Yeshua Ha-Mashiach, the Messiah, the Anointed One is risen for you and for me.
Seek Him. Speak to Him. Serve Him. Expect His return. He is the Key to Life and there is no other.

Maranatha. Come LORD Jesus! We wait for You.

CHAPTER TEN
DEALING WITH PAIN

My God, my God, Why has Thou forsaken Me?" For most Christians this is a familiar verse from the Holy scriptures. Jesus cries out on the cross in agony looking for the presence of His Father which seemed to have eluded, deserted, forsaken Him at the most painful, trying and terrible time of His life. He cries out in pain. His human nature bursting through seems to overwhelm, His God nature. He succumbs to the pain of not only physical torment but also emotional and spiritual suffering. We see here that even Jesus our Saviour, our fore runner, and our LORD experienced and expressed pain in his human form. Pain is not unfamiliar to us as human beings and actually its existence should not be denied or ignored.

Take for instance physical pain felt in our bodies. This is part of our inbuilt mechanism to help us protect ourselves from harm, disease and probable death. If we felt no pain, we would not be aware that something is not right in our bodies. We would sit near a fire and get burnt without knowing that we are in any danger at all. Pain in a tooth warns us that there may be an infection down under and that we should do something about it. Tummy ache, headache and other aches and pains are telling us that something is wrong. So, we can conclude that pain points us to the fact that all is not well somewhere. The most dangerous and mortal diseases are those that are called silent killers. They wreck so much havoc on the human body – silently and stealthily – that when their presence is eventually discovered it's almost too late to do anything at all.

That's physical pain.

Jesus definitely experienced it fully as He hung in agony on the cross at Calvary. Beatings. Floggings. Slaps. Nails driven into his hands and feet. Sword thrust into His side. No doubt about it, He suffered excruciating pain.

But He experienced another type of pain from when He was at Gethsemane right up till when He gave up the ghost on the cross.

Emotional torment. The fear of what lay ahead of Him. The betrayal of a friend. Abandoned by the others and the denial of a dearly loved one.

Then after all that, He looks up to heaven for the Father and the Father…is silent. That must have been the hardest and most painful of all the suffering to bear. Quoting Psalms 22:1 it seems like even the Father, His Father, His loved One has deserted Him.

When Jesus cried out on the cross, "My God, My God, why have You forsaken Me? Did He feel *forsaken; and not only by his disciples, but by God himself?*

Could it be that God had forsaken Him?

How can that be? God is everywhere at every time, we reason.

Yes, He is, and He was at Gethsemane with Jesus.

But He was not present as the loving Abba Father. He was present as the angry Righteous Judge, executing judgement on the One who was carrying the sin of the world on Himself. **Romans 8:32a** tells us that He spared not his own Son, but delivered him up for us all…

He allows Him to bear the pain and the suffering as it had been pre-ordained and agreed together from the foundation of the world. That pain had a purpose and even though Jesus was aware of the plan, He still cries out to the Father in His season of torment.

How do we deal with emotional pain?

Is there any point denying the fact that our souls are hurting, aching and bruised? Of course not!

Is it a sign of weakness to cry out to the Father? Of course, it isn't!

When the soul is weary and the heart is heavy and there is no one to turn to, the Father, no longer Judge but the Comforter and Helper is here.

Are you cast down in your soul? Hurt? Discouraged? Helpless?

Call out to Him. He is waiting to answer.

And to heal.

Shalom

CHAPTER ELEVEN
THE RETURN

Lo and behold, He comes again, Son of God, Mighty King. No longer a babe in a manger, as He was when He came before. Suckling baby, infant child, growing boy, teenager, youth, adolescent, fully grown man. Preacher, Teacher, Healer, Deliverer, Lover of men's souls, Saviour, Lamb of God. Hung on a ragged, jagged cross. Beaten. Mocked. Pierced. Broken. Crucified. Suffering. Dying. Dead and Gone.

But it didn't end there. The slaughtered Lamb is risen. No longer a bruised and battered mortal. No more a baby in a manger. But the Risen Christ. Sitting on a throne majestic, on the right side of His Father, praying for you, praying for me. Moving mountains, healing broken hearts, healing broken bodies, making new ways where the former ones where destroyed. illuminating the darkness with His marvellous light. Not only restoring what has been lost on earth but preparing a wonderful home for us to live forever in heaven.

Heaven applauds as the risen Christ appears. Added to the host of names He bears is Lamb of God. The One Who has taken away the sins of the World. The One Who was dead, buried and risen again the third day. God's own Son, given a name that is above any other name. The name that will be henceforth recognised on earth, in heaven and under the earth, even in hell and at its mention every knee would bow.

With His hands outstretched He presents His palms to the Father God Almighty. Brutally jiggered, the scars are still present even in His glorified body yet they are so beautiful in the sight of God.

"Well done My beloved Son. In You I am well pleased. Your work on earth is finished although Your eternal work with mankind is just beginning."

"As You have told them to tarry and wait for Him, soon My Spirit will soon take Your place on earth. You, of course will start a new work here in heaven. As men pray to Me in Your name, I will look through You to them and answer their prayers. When they use their authority as believers in You, they will be able to do the works that You did and even greater ones."

"As You have assured them no longer will they have to be bound by the power of sin, sickness and other afflictions of the devil. Actually, in your name, the name of Jesus, they can also raise the dead, just as you did."

"The era of the church begins and men and women can now access Your finished work at Calvary and become My own sons just as You are."

And so, as the church age begins, the Father God watches and works over His redeemed creation as they continue through time towards its end. He gives them His written and spoken word to guide them. He anoints teachers, preachers, counsellors and pastors to encourage and empower them. And He raises up writers to decipher and simplify His commands, thoughts and instructions so that mankind can be enabled to come closer and closer to Him in their walk through life.

All the while He shows Himself as loving Father and LORD of all.

CHAPTER TWELVE
TARRY IN JERUSALEM...

That's what Jesus our Messiah advised His disciples to do, after he had been crucified and had risen the 3rd day.

"Tarry (wait, keep watch, expect, abide, stay behind) in Jerusalem. My Father had made a promise to mankind years ago by the mouth of the prophet Joel. He said there would come a time when you would not need to travel down to Shiloh or Jerusalem of any of my holy mountains to be able to connect with Me, because I would have poured Myself out on to you and into you. But you have to wait for me to descend both spiritually and bodily to be able to absorb Me into yourselves.

Tarrying, waiting for the Holy Spirit is very necessary, very much essential for the Christian believer. He has been given to us to help, teach, empower us to walk this journey, fulfil purpose and complete our God given destinies. Yet more times than not, we do not allow Him to do what He has been given to us to do. Our self-will wars against the will of God, the will of His Spirit and we do not wait for His perfect leading, methodology and direction in our lives.

We find it so hard, so very difficult to "tarry in Jerusalem".

Jerusalem here, being our own lives, circumstances, decision making, destinies etc. When we find ourselves at a point where we have to make a choice or make a decision to make a move, when we should stop and tarry, waiting for the Promise of the Father, we are in too much of a haste. We just can't wait. We just cannot tarry. We move on in our own flesh, our own leading. We move without receiving the proper instructions from our Master, Helper, Leader, Empowerer. We thereby miss what was perfect for us, settling for the lesser "benefit", sometimes never ever knowing that God had something so much more beautiful, glorious and fulfilling for us. All because we couldn't wait. We could not tarry.

The pressures of life and living war against us.

"Time is passing me by".
"All my mates are married."
"My friends have all bought houses."
" My classmates are directors in blue chip companies."
"My fellow ministers have ministries of their own."
"Time is passing me by."

Like King Saul, in 1st Samuel 13:10; we operate in an office that we have not been called into and sadly suffer the consequences, because we cannot tarry in our Jerusalem. Because we cannot wait for the Holy Spirit.

Do we need help to wait for Him, beloved?

One of His fruit is patience. To grow it in us, we will be tried in that area of our lives. James 1:4 enjoins us to let patience
have her perfect work, that (we) may
be perfect and entire, wanting nothing. Hebrews 10:36 also teaches that we have need of patience, and after we have done the will of God, we might receive the promise. The Promise of the Father.

CHAPTER THIRTEEN
KING OF HEARTS

There's no doubt about it. Jesus is KING. **THE KING**.

Many of us know Him first as the…
* **KING** of kings. Revelation17:14 and 19:16; hail Him as such and we are familiar with that name, it slips off our tongues as we call Him in praise, worship and adoration. The title reminds us that there are kings, yes, but Jesus reigns and rules over them all.

* He is also known as the **KING** of the Jews, first by the wise men who came from the East seeking Him and later on during His trial, passion and suffering. Pilate asked Him "Are You the King of the Jews?" Although Jesus gave no direct answer, Pilate caused that appellation to be inscribed on His cross. It was such a fitting title because it was to these Jews that our LORD first came. They were the first recipients of His gifts of healing, deliverance and salvation. Sadly, they were the ones who ultimately called for His crucifixion.

- He is the **KING** of glory.

The Hebrew word translated "glory" in Psalm 24 is *kabod*, which means "weight," but it is used figuratively, as in "his argument carries weight" or "the content of that book is weighty". *Kabad* carries a connotation of solemnity and power. Calling God the "**KING** of Glory" means He is the most awesome, most powerful king and should be taken seriously. (www.gotquestions.org) What He says goes!

- Jesus is the **KING** of saints. He is our **KING**, we who have been saved & washed in His precious blood. It is because of Him that we receive the ability to become " royal priesthood" in 1st Peter 2:9; Because He is **THE KING**, we become kings under Him.

- He is the **KING** of angels. They bow to Him and obey His every command. Matt 13:41 tells us how (He) shall send forth his angels, and they shall gather out of his kingdom all things that offend, and them which do iniquity. They serve and minister to Him, their **KING.**

- The books of Samuel narrate and the 2 books of Kings are so named, because of the reigns of so many kings of Israel. From Saul, David and Solomon right down to the last king of Israel Hoshea, the Bible refers to many of Israel's leaders as kings of Israel. But the book of Psalms 89:18 talks of the One and only king, "For the LORD is our defence; and the Holy One of Israel is our **KING**. The LORD God Himself, is the **KING** of Israel.

- Yes! He is **KING** of all. He reigns forever and ever, over land and sea, in the heavens and on the earth and even under the earth. But there's one place that He cannot take true dominion without your permission. John 1:12 reminds us that "as many as received him, to them He gave power to become the sons of God, even to them that believe on his name. To many who have invited Him in, He reigns and rules in them.

For He is the **KING of hearts.**
Beloved, check inside. Is He **KING** of yours?

CHAPTER FOURTEEN
HE FINISHED HIS. WHAT ARE YOU DOING ABOUT YOURS?

Every year Easter comes around again. Again and again we give due regard and remembrance to the death and the resurrection of our LORD and Saviour Jesus Christ. The greeting and response amongst the early Christians when He first rose from the dead was, "He is risen. He is risen indeed!" And yes, truly, definitely, He has risen and is alive for evermore. He sits at the right Hand of the Father God, not as a beaten, broken, bloodied Lamb but as the glorified and elevated King of kings and LORD of lords. He went through the fire of affliction. He finished His assignment. He is for ever victorious. We saw Jesus our Sacrificial Lamb facing His destiny as He rode on a donkey into Jerusalem. Each year we remember that He actually fulfilled His purpose, completed His destiny and as our fore runner has laid down a perfect example for you and I to follow.

First and foremost, what is destiny? What does it mean?

Looking up the definition or meaning of the word, one will come across different interpretations of what it means. One actually caught my attention. The English dictionary states that destiny is… "the force that some people think controls what will happen in the future and **is outside human control."**

Well we know that God does control what happens in the future. There's no doubt about that. We know from **Isaiah 46:10** that **He declares the end from the beginning and from ancient times the things that are not yet done, saying, "My counsel shall stand, and I will do all My pleasure".**

So, it is God that the above definition decides to define as "Force".

What about the 2nd part of the definition that says destiny is outside human control? That is not completely true. Why?

Well, God does have the blueprint of our lives, true, but He allows us to shapen, sharpen, beautify it …**as we wish.** Though He has the final say, we can, and He allows us to, have some input into it. So, for example, I cannot change, where, when and to whom I was born or the colour of my skin, (unless of course I bleach it) but I can take some steps to improve, develop or on the other hand destroy what God Himself had written down or created me to achieve.

Like Abraham, Joseph, Daniel and the three Hebrew young men I could decide to walk with the LORD, stand against evil and unrighteous living and thereby enable God to bring out a colourful predetermined destiny in me. On the other hand, like so many of God's creatures do, I also may decide to ignore God's promptings, and corrections and take my own path, rebelling against Him and doing what I want to do.

Either way we can influence the outcome of our destinies by what we decide to do, walk with God or switch over to the other side.

Sadly, God will **LET** us do what we want to do. He has created us free agents with the ability to choose between what is good and what isn't. **"Ephraim is joined to idols, let him alone."** He declares in **Hosea 4:17;**

How do we chart the path of our destinies correctly then?

The manual for living is God's Own Word, the Bible. He can and will guide us through life with it. Also, He has given us His Spirit, the Comforter, our Teacher, our Helper. He knows the mind of the Father concerning us and is delighted to reveal it to us and help us on our way. We only need to be willing to listen and to obey. So that we can one day say like the Master, "It is finished!"

CHAPTER FIFTEEN
UNDESERVED – GOD'S GIFT OF GRACE

Divine **grace** has been defined as the divine influence which operates in humans
- to regenerate and sanctify,
- to inspire virtuous impulses,
- to impart strength to endure trial and resist temptation;
- as an individual virtue or excellence of divine origin.

Some define grace as unmerited favour. Some interpret grace as the enablement or ability to carry out an assignment. In a nutshell we could merge all these definitions to describe grace as God's given providence to live a fulfilled and perfect existence on the earth – in all manner of life's ramifications.

The Bible uses grace in a slightly different light. Ephesians 2:8-9 reminds us that it is "by grace we are saved through faith; and that not of (y)ourselves it is the gift of God: Not of works, lest any man should boast.

That primarily talks about salvation but it can also mean the ability to do what we would ordinarily not be able to do.

The Bible also speaks in various places of people finding grace in the sight of God. Noah found grace in the sight of God in Genesis 6:8;

Grace here, means he was able to draw down from God, His favour, peace, attention, love, enablement etc because he was a just man and perfect in his generations, and he walked with God.

As Christians grace is given or released to us all in different ways and avenues.
Some are graced to be accomplished musicians whilst others have been given grace to be successful business men.

God has enabled some of His children to be worldwide evangelists or notable pastors, while some serve God in the office of administration and coordination.

God actually gives grace freely to His own people as long as they meet His conditions.

"For the LORD God is a sun and shield: the LORD will give grace and glory: no good

thing will he withhold from them that walk uprightly. Psalm 84:11

And of His fulness have all we received, and grace for grace. John 1:16

I want to conclude this chapter by asking you some questions.

Is there something burning in your heart that you want to do, you want to accomplish, a desire to bring into being some idea, project, initiative, something you just know you were created to bring into existence?

Are you on the fringe of wanting to start something but just don't know how to?

Or you've started but are hitting a brick wall and don't know how to break through or fly over it?

It could be you want to improve your prayer life, or your study of God's word or even to spend some period in fasting. You may want to lose some weight or go on a course that will take a lot from you in terms of sacrifice.

Whatever it may be, why not change your prayer style and ask God for grace, great grace to be released on you and into you to achieve and accomplish what He alone can enable you to do?

Don't go on your own strength or abilities alone. Just ask God for grace.

CHAPTER SIXTEEN
OUR AUTHORITY IN CHRIST…

It is really quite simple if you can get your head around it. We just have to understand it.

God does not intend us, after the death and resurrection of our LORD and Saviour Jesus Christ, to be subject to the antics and assaults of our mortal enemy the devil.
Far from it.

Let's not forget that he is first of all, God's enemy…before he became ours.
God does not want him to win. In fact, he has been condemned to eternal death and damnation. So, the good news is that God is on our side. Every time and always.
After Adam and Eve's disobedience and fall in Eden, yes, we did all come under a curse. Agreed. But as we all die in Adam, in Christ we are all made alive. 1st Corinthians 15:22.
One eternal truth we need to remember is that God Himself put spiritual and physical laws in place and He doesn't override His own laws. He actually is bound by His Word. "So shall My Word be that goes out of My mouth" He declares. It shall not return to Me void (empty) But it shall accomplish what I please, And it

shall prosper in the thing for which I sent it. Isaiah 55:11.

In other words, God is saying, "When I speak My Word, I'm actually sending it to carry out a task and it WILL do what I send it to do. It will also come back and give Me a report. And that report is ALWAYS good. ALWAYS positive. ALWAYS in line with what I please, what I want, what I desire".

"Now, your own word does not have that kind of power, on its own but when I give you the authority of my Word, I back it up with My power, My might, My strength, My authority".

"If you are linked up with Me, as My child, Christ's blood bought, washed, clean and HOLY, I give you freely the authority, the audacity, the freedom, the boldness and the pluck to use My Word, on earth and even to move things in the heavens".

What an awesome mandate we have been given, beloved! Do we understand the authority that has been given to us and if yes, how are we wielding this authority?

The LORD or God does not expect us to be flimsy, flippant or flimsy with the use of the

authority He has given to us. In fact, He will never back up a king who is immature, heady or giddy with power. God's authority in the hand of such a person becomes abused and defamed and God will not permit it.
When the righteous, (caring and just) are in authority, the Bible says, the people rejoice. Proverbs 29:2;

If God did not allow the word of His prophet, Samuel to fall to the ground, (1ˢᵗ Samuel 3:19) the flip side of that information is that God will not back up His Word in an unworthy vessel.

So how do we exert the authority given to us by God through our translation as mere mortals to children of the King of kings?

- We start small.

Rome, it is said was not built in one day. A lot of, if not all our statures in Christ must be learnt, tested, tried and built up.
Building yourself up in your most holy faith... Jude advises in the 20ᵗʰ verse of his letter.
- Speak the word, be instant in season, out of season, in prayer, when faced with unhealthy, unpalatable circumstances, no matter how small or

seemingly insignificant. Do not permit any encroachment on your territory.

- Train yourself to use your authority.

Let the Holy Spirit guide you on how and when to respond and when to use the authority given to you in Christ. In the things of the Spirit and things concerning your destiny you can never be too talkative. Keep talking. Keep resisting. Keep commanding.

You have been given the authority. I have been given the authority. Let's be bold and use what has been freely given to us.

Kings and priests of the Most High God!

CHAPTER SEVENTEEN
ARE YOU REALLY LISTENING?

It's a question most people have asked someone else numerous times during their lives.

"Mom," your son asks you after a day at school, "Are you listening to me? My teacher said this or my best friend did that." He knows that although you are looking at him, your mind is actually miles away.
"Darling", the wife prods through your tired and weary mind as you sprawl flat out on the sofa after a long hard day at the office, "Did you hear what I said?"

"Hmm? Yes" you reply even though you both know that although you heard the sound of her voice, your fatigued mind just couldn't take in the information.

Hearing and listening…2 verbs sometimes used interchangeably but are actually not the same.

Bible theologians put the young Samuel's age at about 12 years when God called him in 1st Samuel 3. He actually heard the sound of the voice of God but misinterpreted its source. Three times he thought it was Eli the old priest and three times he was mistaken. The All Knowing Omniscient God knew that Samuel heard Him. He called out to him to get his attention first at a time that Samuel was lying down and quiet. He tries to get our attention too over and above the hustle and bustle of life and especially when we are quiet. That's one of the reasons why He speaks to us when we are sound asleep in our dreams. But He actually wants to speak to us when we are wide awake too. Face to face, as a man speaks to his friend, like He did with the great prophet Moses. Exodus 33:11. Like He did to Samuel.

Modern means of communication have progressed so very far since the stone age of burning fires and reading smoke. Radio signals, posting letters, telephones, emails, texting and the like are wonderful means of one person "speaking" to another, but nothing can replace a good old hug and chat "face to face" with a friend or loved one. It's still the best way to relate with someone else. And I am of the opinion that God Himself, who initiated speaking with Adam and Eve, the first man and women in Eden, really loves to communicate with man in that way.

"So why then," you may ask, "doesn't He speak to men these days?" Or to be precise, "why doesn't He speak to me?"

Good question. Could it be that He actually can't get your attention? No point in talking to someone who isn't listening or who isn't expecting you to speak to him, is there? That's like a waste of energy. It's better to command the person's attention before you begin to speak.

It's the same with God. He calls Samuel 3 times and at the 4th attempt when He has gotten His attention He begins to speak.

So, what's the morale of this chapter? Lo and behold, God wants to speak to us. "Come let us reason together," He says in Isaiah 1:18. "Present your case," says the LORD in Isaiah 41:21; "Bring forth your strong reasons…" Wonderful! The great and mighty King extends a conversational invitation to us all. We want to hear God speak to us. All we have to do is to accept the invitation and listen to Him. In the morning, in the afternoon, in the evening and in the quietness of night, let's keep our spiritual antenna alive and receptive, listening for the voice of our God. For He will indeed speak. So, when He calls your name, you will be ready and waiting to reply, "Speak LORD, I've been waiting to hear Your voice and I am listening."

CHAPTER EIGHTEEN
WHEN IT DOESN'T SEEM TO MAKE SENSE

Romans 8:28 assures us that … all things work together for the good of those who love God and to them who are the called according to His purpose. When Paul was writing this letter to the apostles under the unction of the Holy Spirit, he knew that Christians would go through trying and painful times and experiences. Even Jesus our Master warned us that whilst we are in this world we will face tribulation. "Be of good cheer" He said in comfort, for He has overcome the world, for us. (John 16:33). We live in a broken world that is manifesting in ways that it was not originally created to behave. Our God is working in us and for us in the midst of this tumultuous and decadent age. He's watching over and hastening His word to perform it in our lives and destinies. (Jeremiah 1:12)

What does that transcend to us?

It means beloved, that God is jealously guarding His plans, purposes and eternal laid down intentions for us. As a Master Chess

Player, He is constantly and continually circumventing the wiles and schemes of the devil to make sure all goes well.

It also means that He may draw us back from the momentum of the path, journey or race we have embarked upon because there is a disadvantage or danger ahead of us that we may probably not be able to overcome. He may therefore, cause a delay in the journey so that the danger is past before we get there.

Another conclusion we can make from Romans 8:28 is that we may sometimes experience pain and discomfort in the process of God arranging and rearranging our lives. At these times we wonder where He is and why He has allowed us to go through…loss, sorrow and seemingly failure.

As we saw in the life of Job God sometimes has dialogue with the devil Himself and Proverbs 11:8 tells us that God delivers the righteous out of trouble letting the wicked come in his stead. Exchanges are made in the spiritual realm and sometimes God permits a lesser loss to avert a greater one. Even our LORD Jesus Christ was an exchange of righteousness for sin, giving us life for death and grace for condemnation.

"Why is this happening to me, you wonder? I love God and I thought He loved me too. He promised me this and that. Why am I not seeing His promises?

These are questions that time and time again run through our minds and sometimes proceed out of our mouths. Remember however beloved, that our God knows the end from the beginning (Revelation 22:13) and in due time we will understand that it was actually so, for our latter or eternal good. He stands outside of time and sees it all, the twists, the turns, the valleys, the mountains, the ditches and the high places. Nothing is hidden from His sight.

And because our vision is so limited we need Someone who can see far ahead and above our own restrained foresight as our Guide and Guard.

We need to trust our Guide that even when things seem to be going pear shaped He is in full and total control and awareness and will straighten things out making them beautiful in His time.

Do you love God? If you do, He will make ALL things work together for your good. Just trust Him.

Shalom

CHAPTER NINETEEN
FELLOWSHIP OF HIS SUFFERING

*That I may know Him, and the power of His
resurrection, and the fellowship of
His sufferings, being made conformable unto
His death;*
Philippians 3:10

It's probably one of the most difficult sermons
to preach. Paul wanted to know Jesus Christ
more deeply and have access to His mighty
power. When we read that portion of the verse
we are elated. Who wouldn't want to be
intimate with the LORD and share in the use
of His power? We all want to. But that's
probably where our excitement ends. Paul
continues in that verse to say that he would
also wish to fellowship in Christ's sufferings. In
other words, he wanted to experience
suffering just as Christ did. He longed to
"share" in His pain, abandonment, rejection,
and maybe even death. That is why when we
get to the end of that verse we kind of mumble
over it and get it quickly and "safely" out of the
way.
I mean, we've been taught and "reassured"
that when we come to Christ all our sins are

washed away and all problems and challenges etc, go with them.

Even when we come across verses like **2nd Timothy 3:12**; *"Yea, and all that will live godly in Christ Jesus shall suffer persecution".*

OR

John 16:33; *"These things I have spoken unto you, that in me ye might have peace. In the world ye shall have tribulation: but be of good cheer; I have overcome the world."*

They are not among the verses we memorise and quote during prayer time. Why is this? Simply because suffering is hard, painful and not to be desired. Is that a bad mind set? Not really. It was never in God's original plan for man to suffer loss, want, hardship, ill health or death. No, not at all. Adam was placed in a beautiful garden surrounded by par excellence. He was given a lovely woman as wife. He had all he needed. But then as we all know sin entered the world and everything changed. Praise be to God for the offering of the sinless Man who redeemed us from the horrible effects of sin but we need not close our eyes to the fact that Christians do suffer all over the world due to its lingering effects.

Christians are and have been, since the time of the righteous Abel, maligned, oppressed, abused, maltreated, terribly persecuted & horribly martyred for their belief in the LORD Jesus Christ.

Do we look for suffering as we walk our Christian walk? Of course not! Do we expect it? Not really. But if we do suffer for Christ's sake we ought not to fall to pieces, become despondent and hopeless. Neither must we point fingers judging fellow Christians who may be passing through trying times and valley experiences. Heaven is watching the childless couple waiting year after year for that much desired fruit of the womb, that terminally sick child or the missionary awaiting execution for daring to preach that Jesus Christ is LORD. If they, fellow workers with us, could endure persecution with so much dignity and stoicism, surely we can endure ours too.

Paul said in **2nd Cor 4:17 …that our light affliction, which is but for a moment, works for us a far more exceeding and eternal weight of glory;**

Like we said at the beginning suffering for Christ is not what we look for or enjoy, but we are rest assured that it will surely pass on in due time as we enter into the victory that Christ has wrought for us at Calvary.

Are you presently suffering for Christ and with Christ, beloved? Take heart. It's just for a time. ***...in due season we shall reap, if we faint not. Galatians 6:9***

CHAPTER TWENTY
FAINT NOT

How big was Noah's Ark?

Answers in Genesis offers us some specifications. It tells us that the ark was about 510 feet long.

In order to put this in perspective we're told that the ark was...

i) Two times the length of an early Boeing 747-100B airliner

ii) Almost one and a half football fields in length

iii) 3 times the length of an Olympic sized swimming pool

Okay so we have an idea of how big Noah's ark was and what a gigantic project it actually was. Let's rewind some 4400 years ago and do a quick recap.

In between the time of Adam and Eve's fall in the garden of Eden and our LORD Jesus

Christ coming down to save us, man became increasingly perverse and wicked.

Well, the LORD God Almighty, the Creator of heaven and earth and all that live in them, was fed up, disappointed, down-right angry with Him.
Genesis 6:6 tells us that God was very sorry that He had made man on the earth. He repented and it actually grieved His heart. He therefore made up His mind that He was going to wipe out all His creation from off the surface of the earth. Everything. Man, beast, creeping things and flying creatures, everything that He had made, except… 8 souls and two of every species of animals. And He was going to destroy them all by water.

As a result, He speaks to Noah, the righteous man who had found favour in His sight.

"I'm fed up with mankind and I'm going to drown them all and purify the earth that they have succeeded in polluting. But I'm going to save you and your immediate family and the way I'm going to save you is by keeping you in an ark, which you will have to build, **YOURSELF**."

Whoa!

God is giving Noah a project here and no ordinary project, one that his life depended on. If he did build this massive ark, he lived. If he didn't build it, he perished. No arguments. No pleadings. No compromise.

No choice here, he just had to do it.

When we are first introduced to Noah he was said to be 500 years old, the father of Shem, Ham and Japheth Genesis 5:32; We don't know when exactly he started building the ark but he was 600 years old when he and the entire family entered the ark. Conclusion: It must have taken quite a long time to get that ark finished. Yet, probably because his life and posterity depended on it, Noah finished the work.

Did he do it all on his own and with his own strength and intellect?

No. God gave him specifications as to what to use and how to build. Noah may never have seen a boat before. So, God had to tell him what a boat looked like and how to build one.

A specific one that would house both humans and animals for over a year.

He said "Make yourself an ark of gopher wood; with rooms and pitch it inside and outside. The length of the ark shall be three hundred cubits (about 137 metres) the breadth of it fifty cubits (about 23 metres) and the height of it thirty cubits (about 14 metres). Place a window on top, a door in its side and build lower, second and third stories in it".

God also gave Noah the necessary man power to carry out the assignment. His wife, his sons, Shem, Ham, Japheth and their wives were the "free labour" God provided for the building of the ark.

What has God placed in your heart to build, create, carry out, produce and actualise, beloved?

It may be something you have already started to do but seems to be taking forever to complete. You may be getting tired of the struggle and stress that it is required to complete it. You may be thinking of giving it up even though in your heart you know that that is what the LORD wants you to do.

A little advice from me is, put yourself in Noah's mind. He must have been daunted, tired and exhausted at times, but he kept on at it. It took years to complete but he would always return to the Owner of the project for clarification and strength. Galatians 6:9 enjoins us *"Not to be weary ... for in due season we will reap if we FAINT NOT.*

Beloved of God, keep on at it.

CHAPTER TWENTY-ONE
THOSE THAT WAIT

Those that wait upon the LORD the Bible says in **Isaiah 40:31** shall renew their strength. They will mount up with wings like eagles. When they run (and there will be times when they have to sprint, dash or undertake a marathon) they will not be weary and even when they are just walking they will not faint. What's the hidden or rhema meaning behind this verse and what does it really mean to us?

There's no doubt about it, as human beings we do get tired, we do grow weary and sometimes we do burn out. Life is a struggle. Working on our relationships. Caring for families. Paying the rent and bills. Even ministry can drain one if we are not careful.

God knows that strength can fail us not only physically but also emotionally, mentally and even our spirit sometimes feels the impact of living in a fallen world.

Day after day, week after week, year after year we may not realise that even though we are not athletes, we are actually running. Short distances sometimes like sorting out a financial challenge or longer distances like enrolling for a 3 years degree course in a university.

The Bible has quite a number of references that are analogies of the fact that life is a race.

In **1st Corinthians 9:25** Paul talks about the athlete who must exercise self-control in all things in order to get the coveted prize.

In **Philippians 3:10-14** he tells us that he presses towards the mark (the finishing line) and finally in **2 Timothy 4:7** he triumphantly announces that he has "fought a good fight, … finished my course, …kept the faith. Hidden in between those verses we can deduce that life is actually a race, a battle, a fight and a struggle to mention but a few. And God knows this, beloved.

That is why He calls us to step aside and spend time with Him, in fasting, in prayer and in the study of His Word so that He can breathe inside our weary, tired, fainting spirits, souls and bodies.

So that He can whisper words of encouragement, secret things that no other man knows and plant in us what is needed to enable us pick ourselves up and continue the race.

When we are fasting, your body is weak and we are forced to slow down regarding the myriads of things we do. We return to a quiet place, room or bed earlier than we would otherwise have done and we are forced to be still, quiet and restrained. Because we think more than we speak, God is able to speak through our minds to us.
"How are we renewed then" you may wonder, "when I actually feel so weak physically"

That beloved is the mystery. When the body is weak in fasting and prayer, the spirit is stronger. Our spirit receives this strength from the Spirit of God, Himself as we pray and study His Word. When the body is subdued, the spirit of man is renewed, rejuvenated and reinvigorated.

The spiritual controls and determines what will take place in the physical. So, when the spirit man is renewed, strength is ultimately transferred from the spirit to the body.

In the spiritual realm, a man's spirit is being empowered and he is able to deal with weariness, frustrations, challenges and hindrances of the flesh. What happens is that they just melt away.

Mountains move and are cast into the sea. Barriers give way. Strongholds are broken down. Chains are broken. Then the child of God is able almost effortlessly to rise up with wings like an eagle, run his race and not be weary, walk briskly and not faint.

That's why we wait on the LORD, beloved.

May the fruit of our waiting remain for ever in Jesus' name.

CHAPTER TWENTY-TWO
WHEN THERE'S NOTHING ELSE LEFT TO DO BUT TO BELIEVE GOD

Nobody was ready to help him anymore. They had done all they could. They all had their lives to live and he couldn't blame them. If they could predict the time the angel descended to stir the waters maybe they would have stayed with him and waited, but no one knew the day nor the time. All on his own now. There was nothing else left for him to do but to believe God.

"Madam, we can't do anything more for you," she heard the familiar phrase and the well-known look on their faces as they tried to hide their disgust of the putrefying smell that came from her leaking body. "We have done all we can do" the doctor said, turning his face away. She had no more money to give any more physicians. She'd spent it all trying to get better. Instead she only grew worse. Helpless. Hopeless. There was nothing left to do now but to believe God.

They'd been in this massive boat for almost a year now. All life and living creatures had been wiped out in the flood. God had promised that because he had found favour with Him, He would preserve his entire family. But they'd been almost an entire year in the ark now with all these smelly animals and food was running out. No sign of land yet. There was nothing left to do but to believe and wait for God.

Four hundred and thirty years had passed since Israel and his family had moved from Canaan down to Egypt. How things had changed since then! The once revered respected relatives of the prime minister now despised and oppressed slaves. Their baby boys thrown to the crocodiles. Their women used as slaves in the most degrading manner possible. Yet the prophecy told down the generations was that the LORD God Almighty who brought them safely down to Egypt would one day bring them out again. The years had robbed them of any strength or ability to fight their way to freedom. Those who had tried had faced the terrible wrath of Pharaoh, excruciating torture and the eventual welcome release of death. There was nothing left to do but to believe God.

He loved her so much, his dear sweet daughter and now even his love could not save her. As she lay at death's door, breathing in gasps and spasms he knew there was nothing more he could do for her. That's why he travelled all that way to seek the One who may be able to save her. "Hurry!" he screams silently as the Master is delayed by a woman with her own horrible problem.

"It's too late!" he hears the familiar cries of his people as they approach him from a distance. "She's dead. Don't trouble the Master any longer." All over. Finished. The end. There was nothing left to do now but to believe God.

Different people. Different circumstances.

The man at the pool of Bethsaida.

The woman with the issue of blood leaking from her body.

Noah and his family seeking refuge from extermination in the ark of gopher wood.

The children of Israel in captivity in Egypt.

Jarius and his dying daughter.

It seemed that there was no way out. No hope left.

And yet in His great and indescribable mercy, God still helped them to believe. After everything else had been tried and had failed, He enabled them to have faith in Him and His Word, that He was able to do for them what they desired. If they could only believe, they would receive. Healing. Deliverance. Freedom. Restoration. Life. And they did believe, and as they did, their faith made them whole. **When all has been said and done and there's nothing else left to do, believe God…**

CHAPTER TWENTY-THREE
WHAT ARE YOU SAYING TO YOURSELF?

Life is a journey. Life is a marathon. Life is a battle. Life has valleys. Life has hills and mountains. Life can be very rocky.
Wow! If life is all that, is life worth living then? Of course! Life is good. Sweet and filled with blessings, it's just that we have to know, not just how to access these blessings, but that there's an enemy prowling about trying to make sure we don't.

An enemy can be physical or spiritual. Enemy means battle. Battle connotes weapons.
We need to have access to these weapons and know how to use them. These weapons of our warfare are not physical [weapons of flesh and blood], but they are mighty before God for the overthrow *and* destruction of strongholds. They are not bombs or AK-47 rifles. There are quite a number of them but the most deadly one, which is given to us both to attack and repel attacks is the word that we speak from our mouths. The spoken word is so powerful and so accessible for our use. That is why the Bible is constantly reminding us and warning

us concerning the implications of the words that proceed out of our mouths. They kill and make alive. They are spirit and they are life. They can move mountains. They can still storms. They can cast out demons, heal the sick and even raise the dead. Because of the awesome power and ability embedded in our words we are to choose to disseminate them with care and caution.

The best way to know when and how to speak is to listen for direction and guidance from the Holy Spirit, Who lives in us. He, Himself does not speak idly. He listens for the Voice of the Father, before He speaks. John 16:13. There is an unbreakable connection between them and communication proceeds freely without hindrance. Then what He hears from the Father He relates to us and shows us things to come. Because He is in complete harmony with the Father and the Son, He cannot speak in error or make a mistake. His information, leading and direction is perfect all the time. And if we listen to Him, before we speak, so will ours.

We live a fast moving, supersonic world and we seem to be always on the go. Even when we are on holiday, the laptop or phone is open and we are checking emails, texts, bank balances etc. Sometimes we have to give an answer to a question or a query immediately. Will we always have the time to listen for His leading before we speak?

When Nehemiah, Artaxerxes, the king's cupbearer was asked by his master why his countenance was so downcast and dejected, he hardly had time to go down on his knees asking the Holy Spirit what to say. He offered a quick prayer and proceeded to answer. "Let the king live for ever: why should not my countenance be sad, when the city, the place of my fathers' sepulchres, lie waste, and the gates are consumed with fire? If it please the king, and if your servant has found favour in your sight, that you would send me to Judah, to the city of my fathers' sepulchres, that I may build it.

Quick question. Quick prayer. Quick answer. And it was a good answer at that, because not only did the king let him go but he gave Nehemiah all he needed to repair the wall. "The king granted me, according to the good hand of my God upon me," he reported.

True, the world is fast and spiralling on and on at a sometimes, alarming rate but actually the

Holy Spirit is even faster. Quicker. Through the Word He is quick and powerful. Hebrews 4:12.

I think the main reason why we do not hear Him speak to us as quickly as we want, is that we haven't actually cultivated the habit of listening for His voice even when we are not stressed or pressurized. In the quietness of a cool evening or under the running water of a hot shower, let's cultivate the habit of listening for His voice. The more we listen, the more He speaks and the faster we grasp His leading and direction.

And then just as He does, what we hear, let us speak out.

"It is well with me. The hand of the LORD is upon me for favour and for good. No weapon formed or fashioned against me shall prosper. The wealth of the heathen is laid up for me, because I am righteous. I remember the LORD my God: for it is He that is giving me the power to get wealth, so that He may establish His covenant which He swore to our fathers…. When the wicked, even mine enemies and my foes, came upon me to eat up my flesh, they stumbled and fell."

When we are going through a dry and arid patch, "He leads me besides the still waters. He restores my soul. He will open rivers in high places, and fountains in the midst of the valleys: He will make the wilderness a pool of water, and the dry land springs of water."

And when we are down and discouraged, "Your rod and Your staff, they comfort me."

Powerful words that release power when they are spoken out by the prompting and the leading of the Holy Spirit, the Power Giver.

Let's listen for His voice & speak out as from today!

Be blessed!

CHAPTER TWENTY-FOUR
RELATIONSHIPS AND CONFLICTS

James 4:1 Where do wars and
fights come from among you?
Do they not come from your desires
for pleasure that war in your members?

What better way to start looking at relationships and conflicts than to examine the Most Perfect Relationship that had ever been. The Eternal Relationship between the Father, the Son and the Holy Spirit. The Trinity. Three in One. Three Persons. One God. Always in perfect harmony. In perfect agreement.

In Genesis 1:1-3; we see God the Father speaking, God the Son doing and God the Holy Spirit hovering and empowering. The result? The creation of a magnificent and beautiful world.

When it was time to create man, God the Father says "Let Us (We three i.e.) make man in Our own image, after Our own likeness…" There was a perfect consensus between the three most powerful Beings in the universe and we … were fashioned after Their likeness.

So why do we fight and war amongst ourselves then?

God's original plan for mankind was social interaction, harmony, love and peace. In Genesis 2:18 God made His intention known. "It is not good that the man should be alone; I will make him a helper that's suitable for him".

So, God makes Eve the first woman and many more people were created by Him as the world began to be filled with people. God's intention was for them to live together in harmony, peace, oneness and understanding.

But that didn't last for long. Something dastardly that had happened in the heavens was unleashed on earth and conflict and dysfunctional relationships began to occur.

Conflict began in heaven in the form of that top-ranking soldier of God's kingdom. We learnt in the prologue how Lucifer, son of the morning was cut down to the ground for rebelling against the LORD God Almighty. Isaiah 14: 12 and13 reports on the judgement meted out to him by and how he was thrown out from the heaven of heavens. He found a way to enter earth, possess a snake and thereby brought conflict right into Eden, the abode of the first man and woman, Adam and Eve. Causing them to disobey God, sin is introduced into our world and the couple began to turn against each other.

"The woman whom you gave to be with me is the cause of this disobedience. It's her fault".

Adam and Eve are automatically separated from God and conflict begins to flare up in the once peaceful harmonious world. It wasn't there from the beginning. The Perfect Being never wished for it to be so. But our imperfect nature will always bring conflict among us.

God the Father, God the Son and God the Holy Spirit exist in complete harmony. They are known in Bible terms as the Godhead.

The God head dwells or as we say in our English, lives, in Jesus fully, completely, wholly. Jesus Christ Son of God, Himself told us that "I and the Father are one" and "The Father is in me and I am in the Father".

A mystery. How could that be? We receive and believe it by faith just as we believe that even we ourselves are hidden in Christ as He is hidden in God. We also know in Matthew 3:16, John the Baptist recounting what he saw after He had baptized Jesus. Jesus came up immediately from the water, the heavens opened to Him, and the Spirit of God descended like a dove and alighting upon Him. Jesus became one with the Spirit from then on.

One God. Three Persons. The Father in Christ and the Spirit in Christ. In Christ dwells the fullness of the Godhead bodily.

The best of the news for us beloved is that as Christ is in us, He brings into us all that He is. Perfection. Completion, Fullness.

We are reassured in Colossians 2:10 that we are complete in Him who is the head of all principality and power. Principality and power here does not connote evil spirits alone. We should remember that before the rebellion of Lucifer and the angels all were good principalities and powers. The great news is that Jesus Christ is the Head of them all, both the good and the evil. …
having spoiled principalities and powers, he made a shew of them openly, triumphing over them in it.

Everything we lost in Eden via Adam, is returned to us in Christ Jesus. Dominion. Righteousness. Access to God. Peace.

Success. Health. Wealth. Freedom from sin and demonic oppression.

We are complete in Him who carries the entire Godhead in Himself. It's a great mystery but an eternal truth, that you and I, erstwhile, earthen vessels could now carry in us such grace and power.

That is why 1st Peter 2:9 tries to reassure us that we are a chosen generation, a royal priesthood, an holy nation, a peculiar people; that ye should shew forth the praises of him who hath called you out of darkness into his marvellous light;

As we continue to walk in the reality of this truth, let's remember that we are Complete in the King of kings and the LORD of lords and maintain this belief till He comes!

CHAPTER TWENTY- FIVE
CHOICES - YOUR LIFE, YOUR CHOICE

I was watching a video a couple of days ago of a nine-month old baby struggling with a major choice of his life. Probably because of itchingly tender teeth he was at the stage of his life when everything within reach would go straight into his mouth. You would watch him crawl towards the family television, pick up a loose detached cord on the floor and immediately try to do what everyone watching expect him to do… put it in his mouth.

"No! **DON'T** put that in your mouth." We hear his father say. Baby stops midway putting his hand down and for a couple of minutes seems to be pondering over a very important choice – to do or not to do. He tries again and again struggling between whether to satisfy his fleshy urge to gnaw on the loose cord or obey the constant command of "No! Don't." coming from behind him. The eternal struggle of choosing to obey or to disobey continues in his little mind. Looking back at his dad, trying to argue his case, sometimes laughing and looking down at the cord in his hand, he has to make a choice. After a short while he eventually does. The cord ends up finally … in his mouth.

Choices.
We all have to make them from when we are first born as babies right through life and up until we reach old age and are called back home by our Maker.
Some choices are quite easy to make while some are actually, as we all know, quite hard.

Our not knowing the future is one very poignant reason why our choice making is difficult. We just do not know what the outcome of our decisions will be. Some decisions have very far reaching effects on us. Choosing a career. Choosing a business partner. Choosing a spouse.

"What should I do?" We find ourselves asking ourselves, our friends, our mentors, our parents, our spouses.
Even when the suggested answers and advice come we are still not sure what is the perfect thing to do.

Sometimes as Christians we know the thing not to do, as some things are black and white. But some other things just aren't. They kind of look greyish in colour. At the crossroads, we look left and right and both roads look somewhat the same. Where do we turn to? Left or right or even go back?

In the book of Isaiah 30:21, God is telling the prophet to tell the nation of Israel, "And your ears shall hear a word behind you, saying, This is the way, you walk in it, when you turn to the right hand, and when you turn to the left."

He is telling him, there'll be times when you just don't know what to do, which way to turn, what decision to take. He is saying listen for My voice. I will lead you aright.

I will lead you in the paths of righteousness for my names sake. Psalms 23:3;

I will instruct you and teach you in the way that you should go. I will guide with mine eye. Psalm 32:8;

God knows we need help to make the right choices in life. He knows that our choices make or mar us. He knows that we are a product of the choices we make and since He wishes above things that we may prosper, spirit, soul and body, He avails Himself to help us make the right choices.

The Bible is there. The Holy Spirit is our Teacher, Helper, Guide and Comforter. And the Voice of God is speaking to us always. Want to make the right choices in life? Be patient to LISTEN for His leading.

That way you just cannot fail.

CHAPTER TWENTY-SIX
DISCIPLINE

What is discipline anyway?

It has a multi-faced meaning. You sometimes think about punishment when you hear that word. At other times you think about getting up out of bed and jogging a couple of miles, going to the gym, losing weight, studying for an examination and balancing your income and expenditure accounts and keeping out of debt.

Discipline is linked with other words. Control and self – control, training people to obey rules or a code of behaviour or ensuring disobedience is corrected by routine, regiment, regulation and direction.

No matter what flashes through our minds when we hear the word, discipline is actually very good for us. As human beings we have the tendency to either run wild or at the other extreme end, be at a completely inertia state of complacence.

We actually have to exert force on ourselves to get some things done.

Like athletes, boxers, footballers and all sports men and women, winning a competition does not happen by wishing and/or even praying alone, a lot of preparation and work has to be done.

Discipline is painful.

In the book of 1st Corinthians 9:25a, Paul is reminding us that "every athlete in training submits to strict discipline, in order to be crowned with a wreath….

You don't just go to the Olympics having spent the previous 4 years eating whatever you like and slushing about. If you want to make any headway at all you have to train very hard. A would-be Olympian shouldn't just eat anything set before him. Apart from the danger of ingesting something that may contain a banned substance, he cannot also afford to slip out of his recommended weight or physique.

Discipline starts from the mind. The battle is won or lost first and foremost in that part of our mind where we exercise our will power. We first and foremost decide what we want to achieve and then convince ourselves that we can. Like the Bible says, "As a man thinks in his heart, so is He." Dreaming it is actually the first step to attaining it.

In Philippians 4:13 Paul was admitting that although he was going through a very trying time, Christ had enabled him to be able to endure, no matter his circumstances, whether he was full or whether he was hungry. "I can do all things", he resolves, "through Christ Who strengthens me."

Discipline creates a war between the flesh and the spirit. The spirit wants what is good, virtuous, perfect, profitable for our entire being – spirit, soul and body, but the flesh just wants a life of ease, no strain, no effort, no exertion of any sort.

While our current circumstances says, "You are okay the way you are, our minds say to us, "My ally, Discipline, will help you become better, smarter, wiser, healthier, more knowledgeable and more anointed. He will help you reach your goal. He will help you achieve purpose and fulfil your destiny.

No matter what time of the year or stage of your life you are, as long as there is life the goals you set for yourself are still achievable.

Discipline yourself.

Strive for them. Get up and attain. It's not yet too late.

CHAPTER TWENTY-SEVEN
MORE ABOUT DISCIPLINE

We concluded that discipline wasn't a word we usually liked to hear but…it is actually good for us. The undeniable fact that we humans have the tendency to run wild or be absolutely complacent compels us to do something about any situation we may find ourselves in. We have to take the upper hand to make a change in our lives. No one is going to do it for us. Inertia (the state of being in a complete position of inaction) is definitely not our friend.

Discipline helps us to conquer this state of knowing that I need to do something but because it'll require some effort I'd rather not bother.

It's easier and less painful to maintain the status quo. Ignore the excess weight and maybe it'll shrink away by itself. Ignore those bills and credit card notifications and maybe they'll stop coming through the letter box. Turning a blind eye to the clutter in my room, my house and the garden shed in the hope that they'll just one day disappear. But living in a fool's paradise and fooling ourselves isn't going to move them away. Until I do something about them, they'll be there until there's no space for new useful things.

Though we were made to believe when we were little children that if we wished hard enough, we'd get what we wanted, we know now that, that was just a fable. Things don't just happen. Someone has to make them happen.

In Genesis 1:1, the Spirit of God moved across the face of the chaotic formless deep and He wasn't happy with what He saw. So what does He do? He takes charge of the situation, speaking life to it whilst His Word creates a new world.

How do we make things happen?

First of all, like God did, assess the status quo. Maybe it's really bad, so we must endeavour to make it good. Or it may be good, but could be much better.

Once we have assessed the situation the next thing to do of course as Christians is to talk to God about it. He is the very present Help in time of trouble Psalms 46:1. Even though we may have some ideas at the back of our mind on how to move on and breakthrough, it's still okay and very expedient to ask God for the right strategy. It's not a one cap fits all situation. What may work for me may not be the best approach for you.

What next? Search for knowledge. Proverbs 18:15: The heart of the prudent gets knowledge; and the ear of the wise seeks knowledge. Don't just plunge into any supposed solution, look for the best strategy that suits you, your schedule, your family composition, your budget.

Then, set SMART goals. Specific. Measurable. Achievable or Attainable. Relevant. Time bound. When I want to get to the end.

Finally start. Nothing's going to happen, beloved, if we don't start. And try and do something EVERY DAY. No matter how small. DO SOMETHING. Today may be better than yesterday. Or it may be worse. Doesn't matter. Just keep on keeping on. DISCIPLINE is the bridge between goals and achievement. We can do it, if we put our entire being to it. Let's go for it, guys.

CHAPTER TWENTY-EIGHT
LORD, WE GIVE YOU THANKS

I don't watch much television these days. So much doom and gloom does seem to have a sad effect on me. Too much abuse, crime, war, nation rising against nation, and kingdom against kingdom: famines, and pestilences, and earthquakes, in divers places, Matthew 24:7, blood shed, death…

You listen to the news and think how terrible the world that we live in is becoming. Like the myth surrounding the tall ostrich bird, sometimes we refuse to take note of the prevailing circumstances happening in the world around us "burying our heads in the sand".

These perilous times just seem to be, well, just too perilous. 2nd Timothy 3:1; Too dangerous.

But isn't that all the reason why we have to give God thanks as often as we can beloved?

Times are hard. People are suffering. But the everlasting God has watched over you and your family for many years and for the additional months of this year.

And why has He done this?

It's not because we are better, smarter or even holier than others. It might not even be because our fathers or mothers served Him with so much fervour and diligence. Or even because we ourselves are doing anything much better.

Psalm 91:7 – 8; predicts and promises that a thousand shall fall at your side, and ten thousand at your right hand; but it shall not come near you. Only with your eyes shall you behold and see the reward of the wicked.

For some reason that we may not even be able to decipher the Almighty God, Creator of the heavens and the earth, Who can kill and make alive, has decided to preserve you and your loved ones throughout the past months of this year. And there is hope and trust available in Him to see us through many more years to come.

That's why we MUST give Him all the glory and all the thanks.

CHAPTER TWENTY-NINE
BABY STEPS

A baby step is an act that makes a very small amount of progress towards achieving something. When a baby reaches a certain age they just one day try to stand up. It's as if for months they've been watching these "human beings" walking around the place. They may notice that some walk fast but some walk slow. Some skip. Some jump. Some they reckon even run. They probably wonder, "Why can't I do that also?"

Then one day they may notice that these "beings" first of all stand up before they start to walk.

They look at themselves. I'm lying down all day. If I'm going to walk, I need to sit up. So, after a number of attempts of sitting and falling they master the sit. "Great!" they exclaim (in baby language, of course), "I can see much further than I could before. It was so boring watching that ceiling all day".

First question of today. What position are you in right now? Lying down or maybe even better (hopefully sitting)? Sitting is good. We get to see more than when we are lying down. We get to size up other people. Watch them making progress. Even applaud them. But we're not actually moving ourselves, are we?

So, the little 5, 6 or 7 month old baby (could be older) sits around for a while, (like we do), relishing in the sitting achievement. But realises after a few more weeks that actually although sitting is good …it sure doesn't get you anywhere.

"Actually, I need to get off my butt, if I'm going to make any progress" he reasons. Just like you and I.

Now we see this little baby who is about 9, or 10 or 11 months old trying to stand on his feet. Why does he do that? He's prompted by something or should we say "Someone".

"Get off your bum and stand on your two feet," His Prompter whispers to him day after day. Just like He does to us.

 "Stand firm and hold your ground," He tells us in Ephesians 6:14.

The little 10 or 11 month baby stands. Falls. Stands again. Falls. Stands again. Falls. Does he give up? Of course not! Why? Someone is telling him "if you dare remain seated, that's where you will remain for life".

He keeps trying to stand, until he finds that he can maintain himself in a standing position.

Does it happen overnight? No. It takes time and practice.

"Yaay!" he probably screams in delight, (with everyone else who's been watching him). "Standing is great. I can see and perceive even more. Wow! More vision is so much greater. My vision is fuelling my imagination. I think I might just be able, not only to walk, but to actually run. Wonderful!"

You know the rest of the story. He does eventually walk, run and maybe even win Olympic gold in the 100 Metres dash. And it all started because he heeded the nudgings of his Maker and got off his butt.

Our Maker is prompting us too, that since we are surrounded by so great a cloud of witnesses, let us lay aside every weight … and sin … and let us run with endurance the race that is set before us. Hebrews 12:1

What race have you started to run?

Some of us may have reached the finish line.
Some may be more than half way through.
The harsh, fallow ground has been broken up.
The road is soft and malleable.

What position are you in now?
Are you lying down, sitting, standing, walking,
running or are your feet beginning to leave the
ground in flight already?

Time is on the move, soon it'll be in full swing.
It surely will not wait for anybody.

So, take those baby steps, if you haven't
begun to do so already & start to run.

CHAPTER THIRTY
WHERE ARE THE NINE?

The story of the ten lepers cleansed in Luke 17:11-17 is not one of Jesus' parables but a true story.

Leprosy is a disease that has been known *since biblical times*. It causes nerve damage and muscle weakness that can lead to deformities, crippling, blindness and isolation. Leprosy in Jesus' time was a death sentence and though in this our 21st century, care is available to treat and curtail its devastating effects, in some countries it still is. Because it is contagious, like all other contagious diseases, people are ostracised and condemned to a life of stigma and degradation. If that is the case today, in about 100 developing countries, you can image how terrible it must have been for whoever suffered from it more than 2000 years ago. They had little or no hope whatsoever. Living one day after the other, separated from family, friends, business, future, they wandered around begging for a living until death mercifully came knocking and claimed them.

That would have been the ultimate end of any one suffering from this horrible disease – high and mighty, low and weak, rich or poor, male or female.

In 2nd Kings 5 verse one we are told the story of Naaman. Now Naaman, commander of the army of the king of Syria, was a great and honourable man in the eyes of his master, because by him the LORD had given victory to Syria. He was also a mighty man of valour, **but** a leper.

He was not excused or exempted from the ravages of the disease and one day would also succumb to its demands.

That was the plight of the 10 lepers who approached Jesus in Luke 17:11-17; As Jesus entered Jerusalem, they dared not approach Him, it was forbidden for them to do so, but having probably heard of His miraculous signs, wonders and deeds they shouted from afar, "Jesus, Master, have mercy on us!"

The cry meant "We are doomed! We have no hope! All is lost! Death is waiting to claim us! Only You, Jesus, can help us. Please do!"

As Jesus sent them to the priest for examination, on the way they were all miraculously cleansed. Cleansed for them meant, delivered, set free, saved from shame, affliction, disgrace and untimely death. Free to marry and have children, start a business and live among their own people.

But strangely even after being delivered from all that, 9 of them, did not, could not or would not, for some very grievous reason, turn back to give Him thanks. **Except 1 of them.** When he saw that he was healed, he glorified God with a loud voice and fell at Jesus' feet thanking Him and he wasn't even a Jew. He was a Samaritan, from a race that no longer had alliances with Jews.

We may not have been healed from leprosy. But we have been delivered by God through Jesus Christ's death on the cross. We have been healed, saved, delivered from a state worse than any disease, affliction and suffering.

He has saved us from hell and eternal separation from the glorious existence that awaits us on the other side of eternity.

With the knowledge of what God has done for us, wouldn't it be a good and expedient thing to raise our voices loud and clear to worship

Him and give Him the thanks that He so completely deserves?

Praise and glory to you, LORD, forever.

CHAPTER THIRTY-ONE
DIVINE ADVERTISEMENT

Who doesn't want to be great in life? Who doesn't want to be famous, well known and renowned? Who doesn't want to be celebrated? We all do! If we were to be given the choice of being a successful well known and appreciated man or woman as against an unknown struggling poor individual we all know what we would choose. As long as we remain under the direction of and submission to the will of our LORD God Almighty, these things are good and much wanted to be desired.

The good news is that God wants His children to excel, to succeed, to blossom. Which good father wouldn't? It shows forth His glory. It honours Him. It gladdens His) heart and makes Him proud of us. Remember what He said about His Son, Jesus Christ in *Matthew 3:17, "This is my beloved Son, in whom I am well pleased".* Jesus had not then finished His assignment. He had not gone to the cross. In fact He seemed to have only just started and yet His Father was already showcasing Him. He declared that He was already very much pleased with Him.

It also comes to my remembrance what the LORD God said about the great prophet Moses in the book of **Numbers 5-8; *"Then the LORD came down in the pillar of cloud and stood in the door of the tabernacle, and called Aaron and Miriam. And they both went forward. Then He said, "Hear now My words: If there is a prophet among you, I, the LORD, will make Myself known to him in a vision; I speak to him in a dream. Not so with My servant Moses; He is faithful in all My house. I speak with him face to face, Even plainly, and not in dark sayings; And he sees the form of the LORD…***
Why then were you not afraid to speak against My servant Moses?"

Wow! What a way to show- case a man! For God Himself to declare that He not only distinguishes Him so distinctly from any other prophet but That He chooses to speak to him face to face. What a way to advertise a man!

What about the second and the greatest king of Israel? Whilst talking about him God said *"I have found David the son of Jesse, a man after My Own heart, who will do all My will." Acts 13:22.*

And though we sometimes refrain to mention God's endorsement of Job because of what eventually transpired afterwards, we cannot but marvel that the LORD would advertise a him so generously and so freely. *"Have you considered My servant Job", He said, "that there is none like him on the earth, a blameless and upright man, one who fears God and shuns evil?"*

If God was going to put you or me on the neon lights beloved, as advertisement for all to see, what would He say about me or you? How beautifully would He be able to showcase His product?

The proof of the pudding is in the eating.

What raw materials can God put in an advert portraying us?

Food for Thought. Be blessed.

CHAPTER THIRTY-TWO
PUSH

Many words are preceded by the word "Push". Amongst others we have push chair, push ups, pushball, pushcart, pushdown, pushy, push over. All these words denote an idea of a noun that requires the application of the use of some form of strength, exertion, effort, or action. If a push chair is on level ground for example, to achieve the required benefit from it an adult will have to exert some form of pressure for it to move and carry the baby strapped inside it from one place to another. The physics law of inertia states that matter retains its state of rest or its velocity along a straight line as long as it is not acted upon by an external force.

It is easier to push on level ground. The position does not change vertically but horizontally. It requires minimal effort especially when there are wheels under the pushchair to help it slide across the ground easily. But this kind of pushing does not climb heights. There is a movement forward but the level remains the same.

If on the other hand, the push chair was on a downward slope all the effort required is a slight tilt and the push chair would slide downhill so fast that unless caught by someone or something on the way the baby in it will be in dire danger of injury. That means it's easier, less stressful and requires very minimum effort to go down that to move up.

But if the push chair was to be pushed uphill we know that much more effort, strength, energy and perseverance will be required. Going up (unless you are in a lift) is so much harder than remaining on the level which you are or going down. Going up means you are pushing against the gravitational force which wants to keep you down. Gravity says what goes up must come down. All things are either rooted to the earth or must return there at one time or the other.

But God's law of rising up and soaring revealed to us in Isaiah 40:31 puts aside His law of gravity.

It declares: "But those who wait on the LORD Shall renew their strength; They shall mount up with wings like eagles, They shall run and not be weary, They shall walk and not faint". God is enjoining us beloved, to press forward, to push upwards, to refuse to stay on level ground.

In **Colossians 3:1** "If you then be risen with Christ, seek those things which are above, where Christ sits on the right hand of God."

Pushing requires strength, energy, force and power that is available for us in Christ Jesus. I can do all things through Christ who strengthens me. If we're not feeling any stretching of physical or spiritual energy, then we are not pushing ourselves to the limit.

I can do all things Paul said in Philippians 4:13.

So can we!

CHAPTER THIRTY-THREE
WHEN YOU JUST HAVE TO LOOK BACK...

It was a bright sunny Saturday in December. Jo had gotten married just that morning. It was the custom in those days to go back to her parent's house to get ready for the evening party holding there. Then much later that night, the ceremonial tradition of her new husband's people coming to whisk her away to her their family's abode.

And so, it was that memorable night. The prayers had been said and the tears had been shed. Did I say tears? I meant wailing. As she's being led away (hopefully not like a lamb to the slaughter), they warn her, "Don't look back! Don't look back! Or else!"

Amidst the tears and feeling of trepidation for the future she wonders, "Why mustn't I look back?"

Well, it was an old wives' tale warning a new bride that looking back on the night of your wedding was a sure prerequisite of a failed marriage and a return back home in a couple of months.

A probable simple and better advice would have been, "move on from the past and press forward focusing on the future."

Oh well, the old wise men thought frightening you would be a better strategy.

Don't look back! Don't look back!

Remember Lot's wife? Of course, you remember her. God had rained down fire and brimstone on the two cities Sodom and Gomorrah because of their evil ways and two angels had been sent to rescue Lot and his family. In Genesis 19:17 the angels warned them, "Escape for your life! Do not look behind you nor stay anywhere in the plain. Escape to the mountains, lest you be destroyed."

If you do know the story, you'll remember that Lot's wife unfortunately did look back and turned into a pillar of salt. Jesus reminded His listeners of this sad story, in Luke 17:32, of the dangers of starting the Christian race and then looking back with the intention of turning back.

Don't look back! Don't look back!

Looking back at most times connotes a feeling of nostalgia or maybe giving up and longing to return to base, when things are not working out the way we had hoped.

But actually, that is not always the case.

Sometimes looking back in time can be a good thing. When your present circumstances are challenging and you feel as if you're snowed under, it's good to look up to God and look back in time to remember how He had brought you out of overwhelming problems of the past.

In Exodus 19:3-4 …the LORD called to …Moses from the mountain, saying, "… you shall say to the house of Jacob, and tell the children of Israel: 'You have seen what I did to the Egyptians, and *how* I bore you on eagles' wings and brought you to Myself." He was enjoining His people to look back and remember.

Reminiscing on days of joy, peace and laughter are good for the soul. A merry heart does good like medicine the Bible says in Proverbs 17:22;

In times of drought and discouragement, looking back down the years to times of abundance, success and breakthroughs help us to give the eternal God due thanksgiving, knowing that He who has saved and provided for us before, is faithful to do the same for us again and again and forever.

It's okay to look back sometimes, but always eagerly look forward into the bright future.

CHAPTER THIRTY-FOUR
CHANGING SEASONS

I don't know what time of the year is it at your end as you read this, but as I write here in England it is spring.

Yaay! Spring has come at last, at least it feels like it and joy is in the air. The wonderful thing about spring is that you may not have a penny in your pocket but you feel like you're on top of the world. You just feel like singing, shouting and jumping here and there. If feels like if the weather is so warm and shiny, it means every thing's going to be alright.

Spring is here and winter has finally given way to flowers, green leaves, cooing birds and butterflies. And thank God, you and I are alive to see it all.

The Bible speaks to us about seasons in Ecclesiastes 3:1 To everything *there is* a season, A time for every purpose under heaven, it says. We all in different seasons of our lives. Some of us adults are at that time of our lives when we are as free as a bird. We can come and go as we please. We may be in University or at the post University stage.

No wife. No husband. And definitely no children. A stage to actually enjoy and make the best use of, for ourselves and for our God. It's a good season to be in. If you're in it right now enjoy it while it lasts. It doesn't last very long.

This is the season when the preacher in the book of Ecclesiastes 12:1 warns us to "Remember now your Creator in the days of your youth, before the difficult days come…" As Jesus reiterated in John 9:4 "I must work the works of Him who sent Me while it is day; *the* night is coming when no one can work".

Seasons come. Seasons go.

Some of us are in the child bearing and child rearing stage.

This season is filled with mixed feelings. We love the role and blessings of parenthood, definitely, but we wish they had grown up to be able to cook and clean after themselves, go to school on the bus and run a few errands on our behalf. We know how you feel but don't wish this season away. It's a time to grow into each other and to mould a new generation. It's a time to teach them how to love, build relationships and watch them learn new things. It's a time to impart godliness and righteousness into a young soul and to recruit a future soldier into the army of Christ. It's a period in which we "help" God look after and nurture one of His own. "Train up a child in the way he should go" He said, "when he is old he will not depart from it". Proverbs 22:6.

It's an awesome season.

The wise man of God, Daniel tells us in Daniel 2:21 that (God) changes the times and the seasons; He removes kings and raises up kings; He gives wisdom to the wise and knowledge to those who have understanding. God is actually in charge, not only of the climatic seasons but also the changing seasons of our lives. He is sets the time for what He wants us to achieve and deliver in our service to Him.

Some of us have left or are leaving the stage where we have to be at the beck and call of these precious children of God. Our seasons are evolving into a time when God expects us to do much more in His kingdom. Praying more fervently. Fasting more regularly. Mentoring and encouraging others. Sacrificing even more of our time and substance than we were able to do before. The children are becoming more independent and able to take care of themselves. To whom much is expected much is required and in this season much is expected of us from God.

Do we then say, "I'll wait until the children are grown up and have left home, before I throw myself into the work of God?" Before I serve in His house as a chorister or an usher or a children's teacher? Should I wait until they are teenagers before I visit the old and elderly or encourage the widow down the street?

Of course not!

Just like the winter season does not prevent us from working and eating, likewise there is opportunity for service to God at every season of our lives.

Samuel began his service to God as a freshly weaned child.

Josiah *was* eight years old when he became king of Judah, 2nd Kings 22:1;

Jesus was twelve years old when His parents looked for Him and found Him in the temple, "going about His Father's business".

Daniel, Shadrach, Meshach and Abednego were mere youths when they stood up for their faith centuries ago in Babylon. While the great leader Moses started his own ministry at the age of 80.

God controls the seasons. Just as winter gives way to spring, so we will also move from season to season. And our lives are in His hands.

I think the most important thing is to make the best of each season. For ourselves, our families, our communities and our God.

CHAPTER THIRTY-FIVE
TOMORROW'S FATHERS

Fathers' Day comes around once a year, in many countries and it's a good time to celebrate and honour our fathers.

This chapter is about them. Not the ones that are already dads but the ones who will become dad's in the future.

So whether you are presently raising sons (or you are raising daughters) this write up is for you. One day your little young son will become a man. One day that sweet little girl will marry one. What kind of man will that be? Good. Kind. Loving and caring. Peaceful. Godly. Hardworking and courageous. I'm sure we all want that kind of man as our sons and sons in law. Of course. But how will you ensure that we get what we want? Are we thinking far into the distant future and making spiritual and physical preparations to ensure that we receive what we desire? They don't just fall into our laps, you know. There's a lot of work to be down to actualize our desire. These are perilous times as we can see all around us.

Drug addictions. Perversion of the most abominable order. Suicide Bombers. Rapes. Murders. Terrorism. Genocide.

It's an evil and dangerous time we live in.

Yes, we know the devil is on the rampage out to destroy the souls of men. True. But should we sit back and just let him?

Of course not!

There is a lot we can do to fight for our land and our world and one of them is to equip the next generation to be able to continue the fight when we leave. To hold on to our territory and resist the work of the evil one, in fact put him to flight.

Do you know that most of our young people have no idea, or have any inclination at all of the war of good against evil and I mean, the correct one. Not the one we see on the TV or in the movies. I mean the war between God and the devil for the souls of men. Because they do not know, because they are not informed they cannot be adequately prepared. And their ignorance makes them a ready tool in the hand of the devil to mess themselves and their world up even more.

That is why we parents and mentors have an awesome responsibility towards these children. And we must fulfil it.

We must start early. As soon as possible.

If we train them and set them on the right path sooner than later, if we introduce them to their Creator and monitor their relationship with Him from an early age, if we lead them in the way that they should go, when they are old…Proverbs 22:6; assures us, they will not stray away. They will not depart from that way. They will keep treading and following its path.

Focusing on fathers, it is our responsibility to prepare our sons to be fine, disciplined men, ready to be presented as great husbands and loving fathers when the time comes. We can't leave it to chance and hope they learn along the way. We must teach and instruct them intentionally.

And what if our children are daughters? As we work out our own salvation "with fear and trembling" (Philippians 2:12), we would do well to work out, "in prayers and fastings", the salvation of the soul of that yet to be known man, who will, in the future, become her husband.

As we have a mandate to train up our son, we actually do have a mandate to our son in law too. We do not know him when he is young and growing, true, but God does.

We may not be directly responsible for his training and upbringing. That is also a fact. But if he is going to become our son, one day, it would be wise to mention him in prayers from right now, don't you think?

That will be like helping his mom and dad along the way, spiritually as they do their bit in the natural.

The Bible states that "the heart of kings is in the hand of the LORD and like the rivers of water; He turns it wherever He wishes, Proverbs 21:1. It means a lot of prayer can fine tune the heart and prepare that little boy who will one day be a young man walking into your family or the family of someone else.

Once a year Fathers' Day comes around. One day we'll be, by the grace of God, celebrating it with a different generation of fathers. Let's do our work properly now.

One day we'll be able to sit back and rejoice in whom our sons and sons in law have become.

CHAPTER THIRTY-SIX
WHY LIE?

People lie for myriads of reasons. Economic, social, religious, safety, romantic, family pressures, political, etc. People lie to deceive others, people lie to even deceive themselves. People even lie for no cognisant reason at all. Even when they know no one's going to believe them they still lie. Just for the fun of it. But no matter the reasons for why people lie, what does the Bible say about liars?

Talking about the new heaven and the new earth, Revelation 21:27 warns that "...there shall in no wise enter into it anything that defiles, neither whatever works abomination, or makes a lie: but they which are written in the Lamb's book of life". That of course, means that liars will not be able to gain access into heaven. And why would that be? Apart from the fact that lying and deception, belong to the same sin family, the Owner of heaven, is called the Way, **THE TRUTH** and the Life.

Let's look at the implication of this reality.

A lie is defined as "a false statement made with deliberate intent to deceive; an intentional untruth; a falsehood…

And truth is defined as "being in accordance with the actual state or conditions; conforming to reality or fact; not false"

One definition is definitely the opposite of the other. One is at tangent to the other. They never meet. Likewise, they never meet in eternity, because the Owner of heaven cannot behold a lie and keeps liars out of His kingdom.

The very sad reality clinging to liars is that many so called "good" people lie. Take a step further, even good Christians lie. Actually, a number of ministers of the gospel have been known to lie, over and over again. Never having been caught red handed they lie again and again, thinking that lying and getting away with it makes them smart, makes them clever.

Lies can be told for years and years to the extent that the truth is forgotten and the lie becomes a belief, but that doesn't make the lie a truth in the sight of God. A lie to God is and will always be a lie, no matter for how long it has been believed. For our God never, ever forgets.

When we stand before our LORD on the judgement day, in the book of Matthew 7:22-23; Jesus predicts that "Many will say to me in that day, Lord, Lord, have we not prophesied in thy name? and in thy name have cast out devils? and in thy name done many wonderful works? And then will I profess unto them, I never knew you: depart from me, ye that work iniquity".

"Work of iniquity" also includes "lies". It's not worth the risk being left out of God's kingdom and having to spend eternity you know where, because of those so called "little white lies". It is the time to flush them completely.

NOW!

CHAPTER THIRTY-SEVEN
WHAT CAN GOD REMEMBER?

Everything & anything. The Bible tells us that He remembered Sarah. He remembered Hannah. He remembered Noah. He will remember you and He will remember me. God never forgets. Even though in Hebrews 8:12, He reassures that "I will be merciful to their unrighteous- ness and their sins and their iniquities will I remember no more" it's not that God cannot bring them back to mind. It's not that His mind is too full of the cares and worries of mankind. It's not that He can't remember those sins and iniquities. He CHOOSES to put them out of His mind. He chooses not to dwell on them, not to allow them dictate how He will respond to us in the future. He is saying something like this; "I know you have sinned, I'm aware of your mistakes, errors and weaknesses, but because you have chosen to repent and make the necessary changes, amendments, restitution, I make up my mind to put your sin BEHIND me. I will speak of it no more and it will play no role in the relationship between Me and you in the future".

Wow! Isn't that great and reassuring, beloved?

The LORD God is great and merciful, remembering our sins and iniquities NO MORE.

The flip side of that analogy is that, as God chooses to forget our sins, He actually remembers every good, holy, righteous deed that we ever endeavour to perform. Nothing escapes His sight and nothing is lost in His memory. For every seed, every sacrifice, every act of kindness, love and compassion, we can be rest assured that God never forgets and returns due reward in the time He has allotted for it.

The relationship we have with Him is sincere and transparent. He is a Rewarder of those who diligently seek Him. His eyes are upon the righteous, He blesses them and His ears are open unto their cry. Psalm 34:15. You meet the conditions. You obey His commands. You walk in His ways and you have the right to remind Him of His promises.

In the book of 2nd Kings 20:3; God had said to King Hezekiah, "Come on, son, pack up, put your house in order, it's time for you to die. I'm taking you home."

But Hezekiah knew that He had been serving the God who never forgets the works of righteousness of His people and so He proceeded to bargain with Him, to REMIND Him.

"Remember now, O LORD, I pray, how I have walked before You in truth and with a loyal heart, and have done what was good in Your sight." And Hezekiah wept bitterly.

Does God forget? Of course not! What Hezekiah was doing was to plead with God to look with mercy and compassion on the way He had walked with God, BEFORE executing that decision to take him home, albeit prematurely.
Outside of Jesus Christ we have no righteousness of our own. All our righteousness are like filthy rags in God's sight. But by the blood and through the blood of Jesus we have been made righteous and can stand in right standing before Him.

Do you know that from our elevated positions as sons, we can even reason with our Father?

"Produce your cause, says the LORD;" in Isaiah 41:21; "bring forth your strong reasons, says the King of Jacob".

"Come…let's reason together…" Isaiah 1:18a, He invites us. Servants don't have that privilege of dialoguing with their Master …but sons do. And you and I are sons of God. Are there issues you want to bring before our loving Father as we come boldly into His presence again today?

He doesn't forget, but REMIND Him …anyway.

CHAPTER THIRTY-EIGHT
SEASONS COME, SEASONS GO.

Do you often wonder if there was cold icy winter in the garden of Eden? I do. What kind of body would Adam and Eve have had, to have been able to withstand any freezing cold snow and solidified ice? We read in the book of Genesis 2:25, that "they were both naked, the man and his wife…and they were not ashamed". It was only after they disobeyed Him and fell from grace that the LORD God had to make coats of skins, to cover them. Can we presume that before the fall man lived on an earth that was evergreen, ever bright, warm and sunny? Could be. We know the earth (which included the both the sea and the atmosphere suffered under the curse that an angry God had pronounced on them as a result of Adam's sin. In His anger, He decrees,

"Because you have heeded the voice of your wife, and have eaten from the tree of which I commanded you, saying, *'You shall not eat of it'* *"Cursed is the ground for your sake; In toil you shall eat of it all the days of your life. Both thorns and thistles it shall bring forth for you…Genesis 3:17-18a.*

Not only does the earth groan under the curse, in **Romans 8:22,** Paul tells us that *"the entire creation groans and labours with birth pangs together until now*" waiting for redemption or in other words for the curse to be lifted.

The earth as it is now, is not the earth as God, the Creator originally made it to be. We first get an insight into the different types of seasons after the flood in the days of Noah. Here God reiterated in **Genesis 8:22;** that as long as the earth remained *"Seedtime and harvest, cold and heat, winter and summer, and day and night shall not cease".*

So presuming there was no winter in Eden, there definitely was cold weather in Noah's day.

Well, since God had spoken the cold into being, man and beast have had to adjust their living styles in order to be able to live through it. Some animals hibernate, digging into the ground and going to sleep for months. Some birds fly to warmer regions. (Some rich human beings do too!) Man himself, you and me, also adjust accordingly- winter wear, increased heating, sensible recreation types, early nights etc. We have no choice if we want to survive the colder months.

As we watch and experience the season change, we must also be wisely aware of the changing seasons of our own lives. Each autumn, each winter should remind us that we are changing too, getting older, whether we like it or not. We are blessed to be able to celebrate our birthdays with joy and gladness, offering thanksgiving to God each year. This is needful. This is expedient In addition, beloved on these annual events we really should also be learning how *"to number our days Psalm 90:12; so that we may gain a heart of wisdom"*.

At each change of season let's remember that another year is slowly but surely passing away. Soon a whole year, twelve months, Fifty two weeks would have rolled by. Four seasons have interchanged.

We adjust to the changing climatic seasons. In what way are we adjusting to the changing seasons of our lives?

I must work the work of Him Who send me while it's day. The night cometh when no man can work. John 9:4;

Or as the adage says **"Make hay while the sun shines"**.

CHAPTER THIRTY-NINE
WHY DO I SING TO GOD?

"These people draw near to me with their mouths and honour me with their lips," the LORD God reiterates in Isaiah 29:13, "But their hearts are far from me".

We know that God sees through us into the deepest recesses of our inner being. He sees the state and sincerity (or otherwise) of our souls.

He looked into the hearts of the children of Israel and knew that their praise, their worship, the utterances from their lips and the sounds of their voices unacceptable to Him. Sounding brass and tinkling cymbals 1st Corinthians 13:1 reminds us, that these are just noise since they were not accompanied by love, the prerequisite for their offering being acceptable to God.

How sad our God must feel when we do not offer Him quality praise and thereby receive the results of our renditions.

What is behind our singing to God?

(1) Hebrews 13:15; invites us to "therefore by (Jesus) continually offer the sacrifice of praise to God, that is, the fruit of *our* lips, giving thanks to His name. Songs rendered as praise is a spiritual sacrifice. And one of the keys to open doors in God's kingdom is sacrifice. God is so very well pleased with sacrifice and He demands it from us all the time. (He asked Abraham for Isaac, He was pleased with Hannah's sacrifice of Samuel)

(2) In song we share in the heavenly praise. We join the hosts of heaven, the four living creatures who do not rest day or night, crying, "Holy, holy, holy, Lord God Almighty Who was and is and is to come!" and the twenty four elders who are casting down their crowns before the throne of God. They are saying, "You are worthy, O Lord, To receive glory and honour and power; For You created all things, And by Your will they are and were created."

(3) When we sing to God our spirit is serviced, renewed and built up. There is a connection of our spirit with God's Holy Spirit and an exchange of power takes place. He receives our praise and we receive His power. Sadness, discouragement, fear, weakness of heart give way to joy, empowerment, boldness and strength.

(4) When we sing, even though we may not see or feel it, wonderful things in righteousness are happening in the heavenly realm. Walls come crashing down. (Jericho's in Joshua 6:20). Mountains move. Earthquakes occur. Remember Paul and Silas in Acts 16:25; Even enemies are defeated as was the case in 2nd Chronicles 20:22; "Now when they began to sing and to praise the LORD set ambushes against the people of Ammon, Moab, and Mount Seir, who had come against Judah; and they were defeated."

A lot of times we don't feel like singing and we either don't open our mouths or at the best we mumble the lyrics along with everyone else but as the LORD said, "our hearts are far away".

Isn't it time to rein in those runaway thoughts when we are singing to God and give Him quality worship?

You just might hear those walls crashing down.

CHAPTER FORTY
TRUST IN THE LORD WITH ALL YOUR HEART

Man is spirit, has a soul which is the seat of his intellect, emotions, will power and they both live in his body. We know that. Man lives in a fallen world state, so his spirit is restricted most times to the earth and his spirit is not yet perfected. It is still growing. We know that too. Man is subjected to the world's dictates and systems. Man's wisdom, knowledge and understanding is limited to what he has been able to see, hear, feel, taste and smell. Conclusion: In order to deal or decipher realms beyond these 5 senses, Man needs a Higher Source of Help. Man needs God. We know that, well actually most of us do. Which is why Proverbs 3:5 advises us to seek this Help and not think that we can manoeuvre ourselves through this fallen world on our own.

There are certain things God has given us the power to do and He expects us to draw on this power, enablement and grace to do them.

Things like tying your shoe lace or combing your hair, if you are able bodied to do so.

Would be silly to ask God to come down from heaven and do that for you, wouldn't it?
He also expects us to go out and trade or get a job in order to have money to feed, clothe and house ourselves and our families. He actually doesn't drop manna from heaven anymore. (Well not literally).

In Proverbs 22:13, *The lazy man says, "There is a lion outside! I shall be slain in the streets!".* All because he doesn't want to go out to work. *He is so lazy,* Proverbs 22:15 *tells us that he buries his hand in the bowl; and it wearies him to bring it back to his mouth.*

He may well be trusting the LORD to do that for him. But that is laziness not trust.

When Proverbs tells us to trust in the LORD…and not lean on our own understanding or depend on what we think we know, what exactly does it mean?

Understanding is not a bad thing. In Proverbs 4:7, God encourages us to "get wisdom, and get understanding. You are blessed if you get understanding Proverbs 3:13 advises and it's better to choose it, Proverbs16:16 says than to choose silver.

Understanding is good but man's understanding is limited. It does not have the full weight of reality. To have full understanding of any situation "*one must possess:*

1) the ability to completely comprehend all possible options and contingencies (omniscience);
2) the righteousness and wisdom to choose the right course; and
3) the power to make reality conform to the right course (omnipotence).
(www.desiringgod.org)

We know that only our heavenly Father the Almighty God possesses all these attributes and so how foolish would it be to depend, rely, trust and lean on our pitiful limited meagre understanding when we could have access to the unlimited understanding of God?

Especially when He wants to make it freely available to you.

You know that as you trust in Him with all your heart, you only have to ask.

CHAPTER FORTY-ONE
PRAISE WILL CONFUSE THE ENEMY

Job 1:20; Then Job arose, tore his robe, and shaved his head; and he fell to the ground and **worshipped.**

I wonder about Job from time to time. Having been blessed by God with a loving husband, sons, daughter and a grandson I know what it feels like to have the love of a family envelope you. To watch your children take their first steps as babies, utter their first baby words and then see them grow through the years until they become teenagers or young adults. There's a feeling of deep appreciation to God that your family is growing and will one day evolve into a kindred.

Do you not imagine that Job must have felt like that also?

The Bible tells us in the book that bears his name, that he had 7 sons and 3 daughters, most, if not all, of adult age. He must have been so proud of them all. Why, they had their own houses and on a special day (could be their birthdays) they held a party and their

sisters came along and rejoiced with them 1:4).
Everything was just great until the devil struck so heavily and Job lost them all.
All his wealth, his family and his health.. all gone in a short space of time.
1:20 tells us that Job…fell down on the ground and worshipped. What a man! What courage! What strength of mind Job had.

And how pleased God must have been with Job. Remember it was a contest between Him and the satan. "Let me touch all he has, let me afflict him, soul and body, satan had asked God, he will curse you to Your face".
And yet Job fell on his face… and worshipped.

If you read the book of Job right through the 42 chapters you'll discover that there's no mention of satan any more after the account of his affliction in chapter 2. He just had to back off. There was nothing left to do short of killing Job, himself. And God did not give him permission to do that.

He ran out of steam. Tried all he could but lost the contest. Just like he lost when Jesus called out "It is finished!" on the cross of Calvary. May he always lose over you and yours and mine in Jesus name. Amen.

Anyway, we see Job in the midst of the intense trial, bow down and worship God. We have no record of Job returning to God a third time. I want to believe that he **may** have thought to himself, "What else can I do to move this man to shift his allegiance from God Almighty that he serves". Job was able to overcome him by His trust in God and his worship of Him.

Going through a rough patch of late beloved? Praise God… with all your heart.

Praise will confuse the enemy and God will come through for you.

CHAPTER FORTY-TWO
NO LONGER A BABE

A lot of us Christians already know this … that Jesus the Son of the virgin Mary is no longer a little babe wrapped in swaddling bands lying **helplessly** in a manger "because there was no room for Him in the inn".

We celebrate "an occasion of His birth" (which wasn't actually on the 25th of December and was cultivated from an old ancient pagan Roman midwinter festival… But that's a topic for another day). During the Christmas season we celebrate Jesus as a little baby, but we know that He grew up, became a 12 year old boy, and eventually an adult. At approximately 33 years of human years He was crucified, died, rose from the dead and went back to heaven, where He lives now.

And though I think it's a great thing to celebrate His birth, we really should take our eyes off the babe and focus on the Resurrected Man.

The excitement of the little babe in a manger theme, is okay for children, babes in Christ and unbelievers but for those of us growing to maturity what should we be focusing on, beloved?

1. Men, like Jesus, are born. Men, like Jesus, die. Because it is appointed unto man to die but once after this is judgement. **Hebrews 9:27;** Jesus was judged… for our sins which He bore on the cross. Implication. All men will die. All will be judged. For the allocation of rewards or for confirmation of eternal punishment in the lake of fire. It's ours to choose.

2. Jesus was born in Bethlehem in Judea, He was born to fulfil destiny. And He did the will of the One Who sent Him. He finished His work. **John 19:30** recounts that **when Jesus had received the sour wine He said, "It is finished!" And bowing His head, He gave up His spirit.**

He finished His great and awesome assignment.

You and I and all men are born with a mandate from God, our Creator to carry out an assignment, to achieve a purpose and to fulfil destiny. Grace has been also given to us to gently prod us, push us and if we are truly blessed force us into fulfilling our destiny.

Sadly though, so many people do not complete or even start the true will of the Father for their lives. Jesus did. Will you?

3. It was a great sacrifice for Jesus to leave His heavenly home to be born, live and die on earth like a common criminal for you and I, beloved. We see a type of it in *Genesis 22:16* ; when the LORD God requested and Abraham agreed and almost sacrificed his only son, Isaac on that Mount Moriah. God was so amazed. Because He there was none greater, He swore by Himself that He would bless Abraham and the seed that came from His loins. If He could be so appreciative of the intended sacrifice of a man of mere flesh and bones, do we think He would hold the sacrifice of His only begotten Son lightly? Not at all. Never.

He does and will hold this great sacrifice dearly and with utmost regard. And those who despise it, sadly, will have to face His wrath.

4. Lying there in the manger Jesus was fully man or should we say fully baby. He learned obedience by the things He suffered *Hebrews 5:8;* He learned to be obedient to earthly parents. *Luke 2:51;* He was obedient unto death. *Phil 2:8*; He learnt to be obedient just

as we are learning to be obedient also. To be obedient to the Father is not something we are born with. Just as Jesus learnt it, we MUST learn it also.

5. Finally although a thousand days in God's sight are like a day and a day like a thousand years, Jesus had to submit Himself to the time of Mortal man. He had to wait for the time of His appearing and glorification. He didn't enter into His completion on the day He was born. He waited for the time of the Father. He told Mary at the wedding of Cana, in Galilee*, "My time has not yet come"*

Learning to wait on God's timing, may be hard, but God's perfect time works wonders. May we receive grace to wait on Him always in Jesus' name.

CHAPTER FORTY-THREE
THIS IS MY GIFT. WHAT'S YOURS?

He was the Master and they were His servants. It was a kind of employer/employee relationship. They worked for Him and it was imperative that He paid them a remuneration of some sort. He knew their abilities because He had been with them for quite a while. He must have interviewed them initially for the roles they occupied. They might have gone through probation period and as the years went by maybe they got promoted in accordance with how delighted the Master was with their performance.

He knew them well. He knew their capabilities, their strengths and their weaknesses. He knew how gifted they were and how diligently each performed their duties. That was why he had no reservations regarding the journey he was about to take. He knew the company was in good hands. Each employee had been entrusted with a leadership role in their skilled department and He was sure they would function as effectively in His absence as they had done when He was present.

So, He had His last board meeting with them. Reminding each of the short and long term goals of the company and making available to each the resources required to take the company through the next quarter to its next level, straight away, He embarked on His journey.

The head of department of production was a creative artisan. Gifted in the art of creativity, he was always dreaming up new designs and innovative methods of bringing into reality what he could see in his mind. Before long he had increased the output twice over. He knew his boss would be pleased with him.

The head of marketing was a shrewd business woman. You couldn't say no, when she presented a finished product before you for sale. By the time she finished her presentation, you felt your very life depended on whether or not, you took her product home with you. She had a strong charismatic gift of persuasion and she used it well. Before long sales of the company had doubled.

As the money poured in, the finance director recorded and banked accordingly. An honest man to the core, he was however so very incorrigible in all his endeavours. Set in his ways, he never took risks. He was content to come into work do his daily job and go home.

He knew the company needed land to expand. The resources were there to buy. The production department could do with new equipment if he would release the resources they required. A number of fresh interns would be profitable to work in the marketing department but would he make the funds available to pay them?

Your guess is as good as mine.

He was just too set in his ways and so his risk averse nature was having the expected adverse effect on the company as a whole. So even though the others were climbing higher, he was still a cog in their wheel of progress.

Matthew 25:19;
After a long time, the LORD of those servants came, and reckoned with them.

He was so pleased with the report and progress of the head of production. He promotes him and gives him a wider expanse of opportunity.

He was equally satisfied with the head of marketing. Married with little children, he commends her for her obvious extra hours and tenacity to double the sales figures in the time he had been away.

With a controlled anger and a grim face, he listens to the report, or should we say, the excuses of the head of finance.

"I was afraid that I might make a loss, so I just maintained the status quo," he argued. "I have gained nothing, but I have lost nothing, either."

"Could you not at least have transferred the funds to an interest earning bank account," His Master asked, "At least I would have had some return on my investment."

If you are familiar with the LORD Jesus' parable of the talents, you'll already know the end of this story.

"Lazy and unprofitable," the Master writes as he dots the "i's" and crosses the "t's" of his finance director's sack letter. "There's no place for you here."

Of course, there was a lot of weeping, regrets and as the Bible says "gnashing of teeth".

What are you doing with your gift, my friend?

I'm asking you today. One day it'll be the Master doing the asking.

CHAPTER FORTY-FOUR
WHAT WILL YOU DO WITH TODAY?

It's a beautiful fresh gift given to you, given to me, by the Almighty sovereign God Himself. An opportunity to step into a new time frame once again. A chance to live some time in a new day that will extend for another 24 hours. Many would have wished, hoped, yearned and prayed earnestly to lay hold of this precious gift but for reasons hidden now and to be unveiled at the end of time, it was not to be. But for you and me beloved, God our Father has bestowed on us the gift of …life.

What are you planning to do with today?

Have you thought about it? When you went to bed last night did you make plans for today? Did you talk to God about them? Did you pray them into existence?

The year 2017, for instance was prophetically coined a year of surprises, pleasant for the righteous and obedient, unpleasant for the unrighteous and ungodly.

What is a surprise actually? It can be defined as an unexpected or astonishing event. That means it's a bolt out of the blue, a source of amazement or a revelation. It could be something you were not expecting to happen or if you were, probably not in the magnitude or timing that it did. May all this year bring pleasant surprises to you. Maybe today will be that day.

There is however a condition wrapped in the prophecy. It'll only happen for those who are godly, righteous, holy, obedient, soul winning, serving the Master to the best of their ability.

Even then, the thing about prophecies is that you have to pray them into being.

- So, pray that they'll manifest in your life without any unnecessary delay or hindrance.

- Then keep watch, expecting them to appear.
- Exercise faith that what you never imagined could happen to you or your loved ones would relatively fall in your lap effortlessly.
- In the meantime, occupy diligently laying your hands on all that they find to do and doing such with all your might. Not slothful in business; fervent in spirit;

serving the Lord; as Paul in Romans 12:11 encourages.

By the end of today, you and I would have used up another 24 hours of our lives. A whole day would have come and gone.
Before we know it, the entire week, month, the whole year will be gone.

It starts with the passing of a single day. Though we definitely did not deserve it, the LORD has given us a brand new gift.

What will you do with this new day?

CHAPTER FORTY-FIVE
THE END

He sits on a great white and shinning throne. Stately, beautiful and glorious in all His splendour. The white is not really white but there are no human words from any human language to describe its brightness. A golden crown sits on His head as if it had always been a part of His frame and His eyes are like a flame of fire. As He begins to speak His voice is like the sound of many waters and thousands of angels stand in attendance of Him.

It's JESUS. But no longer as mankind knew Him. He sits in all His glory as the KING of kings and LORD of lords and it is the end of time. Multitudes of people stand at His right hand and even more at His left. It's the day that the Bible talks of in Matthew chapters 7:23 and 25:31-48; There is great and thunderous sound of rejoicing from the right side of the King.

"Well done, good and faithful servants. Your place of rest has been prepared and is waiting for you. Come in and inherit what has been set aside for you from the time the world was created. You fed the hungry and cared for the widows and fatherless. I saw you when you visited those in prison, caring for the sick and afflicted and taking in those who were homeless. I am pleased with you and I love you dearly".

Those on His right hand go wild with unspeakable joy. It is over at last. An eternity of peace, joy and wellbeing stretches out in front of them. The King addresses them collectively and yet individually – each by their name.

And then as if on cue, there is a long hush and everywhere is silent as with sorrowful eyes He turns to those on His left and begins to address them.

"It was for you that I came. It was because of you I left my heavenly home to walk the streets of the earth. It was for you I died. But you never allowed me into your hearts, into your souls, into your lives. You lived uncaring, unloving and selfish lives, with no heart for the poor, weak, sick and oppressed. Never keeping My commandments, I wanted to know you but you had no room in your heart for Me. That's why I have to say, "I never knew you, depart from Me for you did not accept my shed blood that would have cleansed you from your works of iniquity." And as the Holy Scriptures surely predicted, "There is the horrendous sound of weeping and gnashing of teeth." (Matthew 13:42).

On what side of the KING do you wish to appear on that day, beloved?

Except a man be born again of the Spirit of God, he cannot enter His kingdom. Jesus is the Way in. And knowing God is not only about teaching Bible classes, singing in a choir or even pastoring a church. It's so much more than that.

Knowing God is receiving Him into your life, loving Him and keeping His commandments and loving His people.

Make that choice now. There is a rest and time of bliss awaiting you….and me, in Jesus name.

Be blessed.

Printed in Great Britain
by Amazon